A Heart waits Forever

Betty Lowrey

ISBN 979-8-9919162-2-6 (paperback)
ISBN 979-8-9919162-3-3 (eBook)

Chapter 1

Florence

Florence made up her mind. She would go, then she changed her mind, a dozen times. Why should she care about the place she visited when she was young? She answered her own question. Because that was where she met him, summer vacations, as a teenager growing to college age, where she fell in love with the boy next door to her cousin's home, Safe Haven. Perhaps it was finding the photo as she rummaged for the key to her suitcase. Adam had taken it, after he gave her the heart. She was standing in the snow and he said she was beautiful and they would spend their lives together. He said, I will love you forever, Fleur. But Adam's parent's interfered and Adam married another. Heartbroken, they had spent one last night together, agreeing never to see each other again.

She procrastinated, to go, not to go. If she went, she would stay at the Inn. She could visit Nancy Ann and her sweet daughter, Elizabeth. The business, left in her son's hands would go on. He would take care of the last deal, though it wasn't settled, whether the purchase was theirs. Another buyer had made a bid, but they were told he was demanding and ruthless in his business ethics. Based on that information, Florence wasn't interested in meeting their competitor and the odds of that were as small as one in a million.

Surely, if she went, Adam and his Charlotte would be no where near the small town, called Mosby, nestled in the foot hills to the Eastern Mountain range. It was a land of great potential with tourist passing by, and it was a land of memory and sadness that brought joy in spite of its self. The joy that came from knowing Adam, was the only thing that balanced the agony of losing him. He would never know. In a way, the anger she harbored from losing their life together brought resentment to this day; he had not stood firm in their love. Possibly, the secret she carried within her heart was a sweet revenge, then why did she still feel the pain?

Elizabeth and Thomas James

Elizabeth was on her way to work, taking her brother along to wait tables, in case the two young women were unable to come in by way of the back roads that were more mountainous than where Safe Haven was located. As she left her mother and Jonathan sitting in front of the fireplace, Jonathan asked how Thomas James, her father's son by another woman, had come to live with Nancy Ann and Elizabeth after his father died. "It was a mish-mash of events that brought him to us," she heard her mother reply as they left the house.

All Thomas James had said was, "We've heard it before, Sis. It doesn't change." And then both their thoughts had turned to the rain seeming at first to fall in slow motion but by the time they arrived at the club it had become sheets of ice that made them wonder how they would find the road when the club closed and it was time to return home. "I'm glad we left early. I can't believe people come out in weather like this," she said as they ran to the door. "It's unbelievable. How can that weatherman believe what he's saying? It is supposed to snow later." She repeated, "I can't believe it."

"Can't you, now?" Her brother was laughing, as they hung up their coats. "We're out, aren't we?" He noticed the two girls had not made it in. "I guess I'm it, huh?" For a moment he wondered how Jonathan would take the story of how Nan came to raise him, her first husband's son by another woman, but he heard Elizabeth say, "you mean no one can make it over the roads. We three are it? You think we can take care of everyone that straggles in?"

Joe made an appearance, "Hey, Thomas James, please, come console your sister. She's whining. Didn't your parents bring you up to accept life has its little handicaps."

Elizabeth was tying an apron over the black dress with the two side slits that revealed her ankles and a definite shape to the leg. "I believe you sewed that slit up, didn't you? As I recall, it went past the knee. Pretty sexy, Sis, if I do say so myself, but why did you sew it up?"

"Don't you know? It's what's not seen that's interesting. Now, Start tearing the lettuce into the large bowl and when that's finished, prepare about ten on those iced salad plates. That should be enough. I, for one, can't believe, people will wander out in this weather."

Washing his hands, Thomas James glanced out the window. "Sis. It's snowing, now." He and Joe laughed as she groaned. "She's just missing her man, Joe. She just as well admit it."

"Oh, really. Where is he? I've not seen our number one hostess this fraught, before."

* * * * *

Nancy Ann and Jonathan

Back at Safe Haven Nan finished telling Jonathan why she had taken Thomas James as her son. "And that is how it all began but

Elizabeth knew him first, after all, he is her half-brother. I suppose that is for Elizabeth to tell you. I have to admit, I wasn't the happiest gal on the face of the earth. Then I met T.J."

"Not many women would take their husband's love child to raise when the child's mother died," he replied. "Did you have second thoughts? I mean, I have counseled couples after one has committed infidelity, that's when people become very real in how they feel."

"Why are you being so nice about this?" Nan slumped down on the sofa by Jonathan. "It was adultery, plain and simple. Say it. Adultery."

The flame of the burning wood danced its tinge of red and blue as Jonathan considered whether there was anger or hurt in Nancy Ann's words, but her expression was more of a let's face fact than anything else. "Okay," he said, "it was adultery, still for you to take in his child was a benevolent thing, in my mind."

"Sometimes, I forget you are a minister. Honestly, Jonathan, you word things so kindly. Benevolent, huh?" Nancy Ann grinned, "I'll remember that the next time we are making love. Who knew a man of the cloth could make love like you do?"

He pulled her to his body, kissed her on the lips and said, "Please, don't ever say anything like that to embarrass me in front of your friends or family." She kissed him soundly, watching his eyes turn into lipid pools of want. "I…" he said in a husky voice. "I love you…but either you move away, or we are going to have to rent a room at the local inn."

Laughing, Nancy Ann sit up proper and finished her story as if there had been no moment of lust. She was delighted her new husband desired her. "So, as I was saying, when Elizabeth told me she had visited her father and his new wife was in hospital and wanted to meet her, long story short, Sarah was her name and she died, leaving a little boy without a mother, and I thought, what if that were

Elizabeth? Could another woman love my child? I decided right then I wanted to meet this little boy they called T. J. We set putting puzzles together to the concernment of his father, who was once my husband, and he didn't really trust my being there, as if I might be contemplating some nefarious revenge."

She gave that infectious laugh that made anyone near want to laugh with her. "You know, like kill the kid, set the house on fire, kidnap T.J." She laughed again. "Who knows what he was thinking?" She seemed to reach back to gather the next words. "By the time Frank, died, his son, by another woman, and I were best of friends and Safe Haven became his home. He is my grandson. Isn't that funny?" Suddenly serious faced, she asked, "What do you call a family like that?"

"Knowing you, I call it delightful, but I guess others would say dysfunctional. Anyway," he grinned. "I suppose you fed the local gossip and if T.J. went to school here, it lasted awhile." Nancy Ann was grinning. "And you with your wonderful warm nature didn't care at all, did you?" He studied her, with warmth and caring. "But one thing I noticed; sometimes you switch his name and call him James Thomas."

"Oh, that," she replied, "It's a family thing, like if you say, you better straighten up, or…."

The ringing of the doorbell interrupted the furthering of Nancy Ann's words. Rising, she went to answer. A thin woman, maybe in her fifties, stood waiting for Nan to speak. With the wind whipping icy rain around the door and the fact she had forgotten her glasses, she could barely see and when the woman asked, "you don't remember me, do you, Nancy Ann?"

Nancy Ann could only reply, "No, I don't. Who are you?"

"Your cousin." She saw no remembrance on Nancy Ann's face. "We played together when we were children. I was named after your mother." There remained a blank stare on Nancy Ann's face. "We almost set Mr. Amos barn on fire when we were fifteen and tried smoking. Put on your glasses, you Ninny, as usual they are stuck on top of your head."

"Oh." Nancy Ann burst into giggles. "Fleur. Come in. Hurry get out of the cold. Let's see what else we remember?" She shut the door behind their new guest and reached for her hand. "Jonathan," she called, "You will never guess who I am bringing to see you." They could hear Jonathan rising from the sofa. "Honey, this is my cousin, Fleur." Giving an exuberant smile she said, "this is my new husband, Jonathan."

Ever the gentleman, Jonathan extended a hand, smiled, and said, "Interesting name and what was that about a barn?"

Nan gave a dismissing wave of the hand, "Oh, the barn, there's nothing to that, we were young and tried smoking leaves in the loft of Mr. Amos barn and that was a fiasco, because it tasted terrible and while we were gaging, we dropped ashes, or you might say a burning leaf, and we had to do a lot of stomping. The smell was terrible and that's what gave us away. Mother was furious and Mr. Amos, well, he asked us in a very strongly worded way, to please not be in his barn again."

"Young ladies," Fleur said with a roll of the tongue, "It would please me mightily if you would not visit me barn again. Never, young ladies, I cannot afford to lose me barn, nor me animals."

"It was the thought of our killing those sweet little baby calves and the lambs, oh, the lambs," Nan replied. "That turned us around." To her husband she said, "We wouldn't call Florence, Flo, which would have been the natural thing to do, but there was this rather crude woman we knew named Flo, oh well, we said our Florence was much too elegant to be called Flo and we named her Fleur, you know like a flower." She gave Florence a quick glance. "He doesn't get it but eventually he will. Anyway, I never tried smoking again, did you?"

"No, I didn't, otherwise by now I'd have bad lungs."

"So, are you just passing through or here to stay awhile?" Nan was studying her like a doting mother.

"I checked in to Mosby's Inn and came to visit you." Fleur's smile held a glimpse of sadness. Nancy Ann was not lost to it. "Time has stood still in Mosby and yet, there are improvements."

"Yes, a couple of new business to keep the native lives flowing and by that, I mean they don't have to leave for big city now, as we did." Jonathan was giving his wife undivided attention. "I went to Florida last year for the winter and that's where I found Jonathan." They smiled together. "And my life will never be the same. I awake every morning to joy I always heard was there, but now, I know it." Turning to Florence, she asked, "Do you have that joy, Fleur, or are you searching?"

Caught off-guard by the question, Fleur replied. "I don't know, Nan. Maybe I am searching."

It was nine o'clock when Florence left for the Mosby Inn. Dinner was enjoyable as the two reminisced over the times Florence visited Safe Haven under the guidance of her beloved aunt and cousin. Jonathan found the two lively in conversation, but he also sensed some things were left unsaid.

"She knew all the places we should go, whether Auntie allowed us to, or not, but she kept us safe," Florence said in leaving. "I love you, Cuz. Nice to meet you, Jonathan. You two give me hope." Florence glanced beyond the porch. "My gracious, it seems the rain has turned to ice. I hope the road to the Inn doesn't give me any problem."

"Does your car have four-wheel drive?" Jonathan was relieved when she nodded, but still he stepped out to investigate the weather.

"It's not that bad, yet, but if it continues through the night, tomorrow will be another story." Once, Florence drove away, he returned to find Nancy Ann gazing into the fire.

"Why do I sense there's more to this story than either of you brought to the surface?" Jonathan asked.

"Because there is." Nancy Ann paused as he threw another log on the fire. "There's a love story, bound tightly in Fleur's heart, I know it, but I cannot do justice to the telling."

"Try me," he said. "I'm a good listener."

"Do you agree, many things from the past stay in our memory even when we wish to forget them?"

"I do." Jonathan nodded, settling down to listen as Nancy Ann seemed to reach back in time.

"There was a gentle young man here in Mosby, that at one time promised Florence his world would become her own, if she would say yes to marrying him. You might say he promised her the world. Of course, she was smitten by his good looks and perfect manners and yes, she loved him." When she paused to consider how to say the remaining part of the story, Jonathan interrupted.

"Your words imply he is still here, but their lives were never intwined."

She grinned, "Nice choice of words, Padre. We dared not mention his name. I'm not sure what she knows of his life, presently, whether he is dead or alive. Possibly, he is still here, in Mosby."

Jonathan raised an eyebrow, but she didn't give that information. "What happened?"

"His family was wealthy. No one knows why they chose to leave New York to buy property and reside in this small-town atmosphere, when we were informed, they had been the whirl of society, coming here no one could do what his parents did, in terms of endowments, grants for graduating seniors, things like that to help further educate or attend college," she saw the light of his eyes, "You have seen this many times, I'm sure. It is as it is. Fleur met him the summer she was thirteen. He was sixteen. My mother would not agree to Fleur dating while in her care, but we could play at the beach all day long if we were together, me being the chaperone, I was young, as I said, and didn't know what to make of it."

"I am of the understanding this continued to college age. Between Florence and her young man."

"Until the year friends of the parents came to visit and brought their daughter to meet Fleur's young man." Nancy Ann took a deep breath as if it was painful remembering. "It was usually fall, when they arrived, as our foliage is beautiful here during fall, that meant the two young people were thrown together for say, October Fest or Thanksgiving, which meant they knew each other well. Fleur always left after summer vacation to begin a new year of school or, later, college."

"But something changed the course of lives of the three, what was it?"

"The daughter of his father's friend came up pregnant and needed a husband, and guess who was pick of the litter?"

"Surely not Fleur's young man?" Jonathan was puzzled. "Parents don't do that, now, do they?" He sighed. "You mean like an arranged marriage, except it wasn't his baby?"

"But those were different times. Families were not forgiving, nor did they want others to know their shame if a daughter came up pregnant. Something like that, we never heard the truth of the story. Fleur was miles away in Indiana, some little college town with more church steeples than honkey-tonk bars and this little piece of fluff, richer than a dog has fleas got her man."

A quick grin crossed Jonathan, but his eyes tightened as he asked, "Can you imagine the heartache?"

"That's not the half of it." Remembering, Nan closed her eyes tight as she shook her head. "Fleur and the love of her life managed a rendezvous for a one-night stand, mind you this is after the wedding announcement was made, invitations sent out and napkins printed with their names that Fleur meets him somewhere halfway between her college and his. She was older than me, enough to finish first year as he was finishing last year of college," pain for her friend was refreshed enough Jonathan saw it on her face. "He never knew that one time with Flo. She was pregnant." Nan looked up to the ceiling. "Flo gave birth to a little boy. She made us, my mother and me, promise we would not tell anyone. Even Elizabeth doesn't know. Had she not shown up this evening, I would never have told you."

"How did her parents handle it and his, this was their flesh and blood grandchild."

"As I said, they were never told. The only people who know in this little town would be me and my mother." She sighed. "Who needed to know? Florence took a job in New York, of all places where the father of her child was born. She was away from family. She gave her son, his father's name and to this day there is no way he would know." For a minute she appeared quite thoughtful. "Is there?"

"Don't ask me? I was wondering. What about Fleur's love, since you haven't given him a name?"

"You mean, did the family friend's daughter have her baby and did they stay together?"

He was nodding. "Yes, I've had a few stranger than life family stories to deal with, but this one makes me feel sad. A set of parents decide their children's future and unless the milk of human kindness ran deeper than in most of us, I can't see something so important as marrying the love of your life should be disrupted by some outland-ish whim of a set of parents." He stood, hands in pockets, jingling coins as he was known to do when he was unsettled, which was rare but did happen. "Well, it saddens me. I hope each person found happiness because that would be a huge disappointment."

"I know, I cried with Fleur over the telephone. She no longer came to Mosby for any reason, except to attend Mother's funeral, but she arrived and left the same day and until today she hasn't set foot in this town." Nan was pacing the floor. "Her story was as sad as mine and, in both children played a major part in the decisions we made along the way. Florence said he was a beautiful boy, growing up and she thanked God every day she had him. She came close to marrying twice but found she couldn't go through with marrying someone she wasn't sure she loved enough to spend life."

"Where is he now? The parent's son?"

"After the marriage, staged here in Mosby, not in New York where it might have embarrassed the bride's parents, it was here because the truth would never be known, Mother and I would never tell it. He was scuttled away to a very lucrative job under the new father in law's prescience."

"Then," Jonathan said wisely, "prescience defined as a dangerous path; the way you are telling me, his family came from a social life of no rival comparison; they left a bustling city life that was prosperous and generated great wealth and gave that up to live in a village by comparison to a thriving metropolis," he gave her a piercing glance, "you did say they were wealthy. There is possibly one explanation, the so-called friend whose daughter needed a husband had something damaging on the young man's father. The yearly visits were but a sham, either to further instill shame upon their son-in-law's family or they were adding to their wealth."

Wrapped in his own thoughts and pacing slowly around the room, Jonathan turned, concerned when he heard Nancy Ann gasp. "I never thought of that and I'm certain Florence didn't either. She would have told me." She stopped Jonathan in his walk, her hands on his arms, "Jonathan, are people that evil they would ruin the lives of three young people and sadden the young man's parents?"

Jonathan folded his lanky body onto the sofa and pulled Nancy Ann onto his lap. "Sweetheart, in my days of pastoring a church I have seen a lot of ugliness." Weary, he touched her forehead where a strand of hair had fallen across her eyes. "There are people who will do anything to save themselves, straddle the fence or cross it completely to gain wealth or save themselves from shame. What could I possibly know about these people? I was dissecting the story to see where an answer might lay. Forgive me."

"There is nothing to forgive. I gave you this concern and you took it to heart to help me because you saw I felt Fleur's sadness. It will be hard on her staying in this town. If there had been an extra room I would have offered, but with Thomas James and Elizabeth having their own rooms…it was not my place."

He smiled, "and now that she is marrying Derek, what are your plans. Will they move in here?"

"I don't know. I hate to see Safe Haven closed again, sheets of plywood over the window, all that." She laid her head on his shoulder. "You are such a comfort. Have I told you for the hundredth time today how much I love you."

"No, you haven't. I'm waiting." He glanced down, "Whose tired, now?" He teased. "I would carry you up the stars, but our room is just down the hall on the first floor. Wasn't that kind of Elizabeth to give it up?"

"Ha. Does it matter. Every night she and Thomas James have their talks laying with their feet dangling off the side of the bed and next morning Elizabeth is wound tight in the top cover, and he is drawn up in a ball like a freezing baby."

"And you love it. They are respectful of being brother and sister. You raised them well."

"Yes, I do." She rose off his lap, taking his hand to pull him up and said, "Tonight, just hold me."

"I will." He said, trying to jiggle his eyebrows, but as tired as he was it was a wasted effort and they both laughed as they glanced at the clock. "It's almost midnight. Let's hurry and get the light off and pretend we are asleep when the kids come home."

Chapter 2

Florence

Florence returned to the Inn, noticing where there had been only three cars in the parking lot when she left, now, there were at least a dozen. She heard a man and his son in conversation with the lady behind the counter, occasionally his voice rose to a higher pitch as he grumbled. "What do you mean there's no water? Doesn't a town this size realize problems do arise and a motel, of all establishments should keep a supply. I never heard of such."

"Sir, we are at the end of the road, so to speak. That's why people come here, for peace and quiet and yes, sir, we are caught in a predicament, but there has been a problem with trucks making delivery due to the icy conditions of the roads."

"Wait a minute. You are just now getting the weather."

"Yes sir, but we are located between Atlanta and Nashville, and they have had weather all week."

"Isn't there a grocery store in this one-horse town?"

She was shaking her head. "No, Sir, possibly one place is still open that might have water, for drinking. Currently, we do have a reserve to flush toilets or take showers. If you would like to drive up the hill, there is a restaurant, or I will refund your money for the room, and you can seek shelter elsewhere."

"That's not my problem. It is yours. You go," he glared at her.

14

"I can't leave the desk, Sir." She was glancing around to see if anyone would offer, but everyone seemed to be slipping out the door to their own room.

"We are not going back out on that road," the man snapped, yanking the key from her hand.

Florence stepped up to the counter. "Are you talking about roads worse than what's out front?"

"Well, there is a slight incline to the Club, but if you went now, if you have four-wheel drive."

"Why do you think the Club, as you call it, might have water suitable for drinking?"

Perplexed and worn from the man's behavior, the young woman replied, "Well, it's Joe, and he always seems to order more than the club needs and he always lets us buy or borrow."

"That's strange."

"Well, maybe, you'd just have to know Joe." Looking for a sign of hope, she asked, "Are you thinking of going?"

"Can you call this Joe and tell him I'm driving up?"

"Ma'am, I tried the phone. It is out. Could you try your cell?"

* * * * *

Surely, she was crazy. Who did she think she was and why was she driving up an unknown road to bring bottled water back to an inn full of grumpy people who like herself had forgotten to bring their own? Well, one grumpy irritable man, the others had merely slunk out the door to their unknown rooms. To say the road was a slight incline up a hill was a misspoken set of words. It was horrendous. At least that's what she thought when the Jeep fish-tailed and gained ground just before she slid to one side into the roots of a huge oak tree. Lord, just get me out of this one and I promise I will think things through the next time and that grumpy man can be the hero.

If things were normal, she could just make a call, but no, there was no signal. How foolish could a fifty-six-year-old woman be? Make that fifty-seven in another month. February the fourteenth to be exact. It seemed an hour, but in reality, was fifteen minutes from the time she left the Inn to pull into the Club, as the girl at the desk called it, well, young woman of say thirty, I made it, she whispered as she pulled the hood of the coat over her head and stepped out onto the icy pavement. Nope, that would not do. Back in the Jeep, she started it again and pulled right up to the door and stepped out onto a horsehair matt that led inside the establishment.

A lovely young woman in a smart looking black dress came to meet her. "Ma'am, we are closing."

"That's all right, Dear, I'm from the Inn at the bottom of the hill and the lady at the desk sent me up to ask Joe if he could spare a few cases of bottled water."

The young woman laughed. "Joe," she called toward the back. "Can you come out here?"

The first person to appear was hidden behind a stack of clean plates, but enough of him revealed to make her think if that was Joe, he was a mighty young proprietor, but he was followed by a muscled man wearing a chief's hat and a white apron over what appeared to be a shirt one usually wore with a tuxedo, justified by a pair of black slacks with a band running down the side seams. He noticed her appraisal. A huge grin broke across his face. "You like?" He asked, spinning around. "It was supposed to be a festive occasion here, but they've all left. What can I do for you? I'm Joe."

"I'm from the Inn…and…"

"Let me guess," Joe interrupted. "Diedre sent you up to buy, beg or steal bottles of water?"

"How did you know?"

"Every year, when I order, I try to remember to add a few cases, even if we have a mild winter, we still have a snow storm or two and Deidre's boss is known for going to the sunshine state and leaving her to fend for the Inn, by herself. What do you think, T.J.," he asked turning to the young man. "Shall we load up a few cases to send down the hill?" He glanced Florence way again, "I hope you are driving a Hummer."

"Nope, I'm not." He was waiting. "A Jeep and I'm parked about as close to your front door as I can get without knocking down the poles to the awning."

"Yeah?" Joe grinned, the crinkles at the corners of his eyes making her smile. "Okay, T.J., let us load up this lady's Jeep. We will try for eight cases."

Florence backed up to the high counter, she guessed worked as a secondary bar when needed, and looked around. As Joe said, everyone had left except for one table in the far corner held a gentleman that seemed to be waiting either for someone, perhaps Joe. She had noticed a new looking pickup truck out front; she had a feeling he was the owner. It was dark where he was sitting, but when after a while no one joined him, she realized he was alone. He was tall, maybe sixty, she wondered if he was beginning to gray as the light flashing in the front sometimes gave a glimpse of his features as it made its round, and he made her think…her heart twist at the memory. Why would she make that comparison? Because she was in their town, the place where she met him all those years ago and still the thought of him made her heart ache.

You are not only crazy for driving up here, but you are also stupid to remember something from the past that hurts you even now. Stop it. Stop it. She turned to stare out onto the dark night, watching the pavement turn white as the light made its rounds. Why did you turn off the main highway? You told yourself you could handle the business part of everything. Now you are curious. And Nancy Ann? You didn't even know she was in Mosby, or did you intend to thrust the knife once more into your heart? Didn't it die long ago? Didn't you die a thousand times knowing he married another? Wasn't that enough?

"Ma'am? Ma'am?" She realized Joe was standing in front of her. "You are ready to go. Be careful."

"Do I pay?"

"Did Deidre' give you money?" His words sound almost disbelieving. She shook her head. "I thought not," Joe said. "Be safe." And he headed toward the back where she believed the kitchen was located.

She was aware the gentleman followed her out and waited until she was out of the drive and headed toward the Inn. Funny, she had heard him cough. Just a slight cough, and that too, reminded her… she had to turn loose of those memories. No need losing her mind when she had been able to stand firm all these years. She had kept her word. Lights came on behind the Jeep. So, he was the one behind her. He was about the right height, his way of sitting had not been lost either, head slightly turned as if reading the world. She had to laugh at her own silliness, otherwise, she might cry. But when she made entrance to the Inn, he stopped and waited until she parked close and walked inside. Evidently, he was a gentleman. She wondered why he was alone at the Club.

Deidre' thanked her profusely, saying, "If you don't mind leaving your keys, I'll bring in the water."

"What? You don't have any help for that, either?"

"No Ma'am."

"Do you have maids coming in the morning to clean the rooms?"

"Hope so."

"I'll be right back. I'll change into denims and help unload the cases of water."

She thought she saw tears in Deidre's eyes but hurried to her room to change. The man who had been complaining was coming down the hall. For some reason, the indignity of man, this one was bruising her usually calm nature. "I went up the hill for Deidre, at the desk, and the owner of the Club sent down eight cases of bottled water. Now, she and I must unload them."

He gave her a squint-eyed look as if to say, what do you want me to do about it?

To her surprise he and a teenage boy were waiting when she returned. He didn't say a word but followed her to the Jeep and when she opened the back, they carried the water inside, two cases at a time. Deidre' smiled and Florence praised them as though she had not previously held them accountable for the sins of the world. That will teach me, she thought, or will it?

She awakened the next morning to voices in the hall. The high-pitched tone of a child said, "It's nowing. We can build a no-man."

A mother figure replied "Snow. Noah, say snow."

"A no-man, Momma."

She found a bleary-eyed Deidre trying to fill a huge pot with sausage-gravy, fastening a lid on top that left room for the ladle to be lifted from within. "That's quite an invention," she offered. "Are you also the cook?" Near tears, Deidre' merely nodded as she pointed to an empty plate of biscuits. "What can I do to help?" Deidre' was at a loss for words.

Florence saw a box of latex gloves on one end of the counter and choosing a pair walked into the kitchen where a buzzer on the stove was ringing. Opening the oven door, she brought out fresh biscuits, sat them a moment on the counter while she tied an apron around her waist and then joined Deidre' at the serving table. "Where is the jelly kept? The bowl is empty." Deidre' pointed to a cabinet at the end of the room with one large drawer where she found the small packages, along with condiments of salt and pepper. Once more, close to Deidre, she whispered, "has housekeeping arrived?" Deidre' shook her head, not meeting Florence eyes.

It was what it was. She was a fool and this Inn, was losing its fight against time.

"Aren't you a handy helper?" The voice of the complaining man, was behind her. She turned, thinking, he has his nerve, but he gave her a half-smile and said, "looks like we are stuck here a few days. They say the way out is too dangerous to travel until they can get the snowplows in. Who knew it would snow on top of that ice? Too bad, but we will make the most of it. What can I do to help?"

Deidre' had disappeared to the front desk. "I do not know. I just try to see what is needed. Does that sound like a plan?" He wasn't too sure she would be nice, but she sensed he was trying to make amends and she could play the game. "It appears, Deidre's boss has gone to the Sunshine state and left her to fend for herself while she runs his business; that is according to the man where I picked up the bottled water. I don't think she had any rest last night and now the help who are supposed to clean the rooms have not made it in. What is the best plan for that, in your opinion?"

"Let me handle it," he said. Her eyes must have given away her concern. He laughed, and that made her more uneasy. "Listen up, everyone," he said. "Our host of this Inn has a bit of a problem, but I think we can help her out a little. Housekeeping cannot make it in today, maybe not tomorrow, either. How about we all have a hand at making our own beds, if you want it made, and take care with the trash in your rooms and lets all see if we can get through this weather situation without too much grumbling. I gotta tell you, last night I was tired and in the worst mood ever and I complained, and I am sorry for it. So, today, I've gotta do penance. I hope you will do the same. Deidre' is just one person. Her boss left it all up to her and went his merry way to the Sunshine state. How do you like that? Don't suppose any of you ever had a boss like that?" There was laughter and a few hand claps. "Thought not," he said.

Everything went well until the man she thought of as Mr. Grumpy decided along with his son, they could make it to the fenced area that contained the large lid trash cans the Inn used to store trash from the rooms until pick up. He brought his son back with blood running down his hand where he had tried to jump the locked gate to the fence not realizing it was further contained by wire on the inside.

"I think he found the only piece of wire that had been cut loose and it has practically ripped to the bone," his father said. "I don't know if there's a doctor in this little village, or not."

"There's not," Deidre' replied. She was fighting to stay on her feet, blood always made her feel squeamish. The quickest route to not fainting was the kitchen. She turned toward it.

Florence was taking in the whole of the matter. The boy was bleeding profusely, and she wondered if he had severed a vein, but it wasn't spurting so hopefully it wasn't an artery. "Raise your arm," she said, "Dad sit him in the chair over there, If Deidre doesn't return with supplies I will go to my vehicle and see if I have a kit. I'm going to hand you one of those plastic bags I saw in the kitchen in a box. I want you to hold it firmly over the cut, to control the bleeding." She left long enough to see Deidre's struggle and returned with the bag. "Turn the bag wrong side out and place over the boy's wrist," she said, but he was too slow. Doing it herself, she then left his father holding it as she had said. Deidre was in the doorway trying to make a come-back.

"Do you have a first aid kit? You are supposed to." Deidre' blinked and headed to the front. Florence followed, realizing the girl was in a state of shock; careful lest she slip she opened the door; leaving the Inn she crossed to where the Jeep was parked, glad that due to the water delivery the previous night the Jeep was close. She never traveled without her own kit.

Once she was back by the boy's side, she asked, "What's your name?"

"Terence."

"How old are you?" Florence opened her kit, as none other seemed available and began to clean the cut with a bottle of distilled water first. "This may burn," she said, as he flinched and turned a bit paler. But not as much as what comes next. How old did you say?"

"Fifteen."

"Is your mother in the room? Do we need to call her to make you feel better?"

"No," he said, gloomier than she expected. "It's just me and Dad." He sensed she was waiting for more information.

"I need to know when you had your last tetanus shot."

"Mom died," he said. "Dad will remember." He gave his dad a pleading look.

"He gets into a few scraps, now and then." The grumpy one appeared worried. "If I recall he had one last Spring. Tournament wasn't it, Son?"

"Yeah, that was Winter Tournament, Dad."

"You play Basketball?"

"How did you know?" He seemed to loosen up a bit. She had cleaned the wound, with water to wash out any debris, and then betadine and applied an antibiotic creme with a non-adhesive patch across the top and was now wrapping a white bandage around his wrist.

"Your tall. I knew a young man that played basketball. He was six-three, and if I'm not mistaken you've already reached six feet, haven't you?"

"Yes, Ma'am." He tried to stand but slid back into the chair.

"You'll be a little lightheaded after losing the blood but I believe you will be all right, if there are no games for a week."

He grinned. "There are not. Dad was taking me to a game in Atlanta, but I guess we will miss it."

She patted him on the shoulder. "I'm sorry you will miss the game and I'm sorry you have lost your mother." She looked him straight in the eyes. "But I believe you will remember the good times you had with her and do all right. She would want you to. I believe the wound bled enough to cleanse itself."

"Thank you," he said, as his dad stepped forward and laid a hand on the other shoulder.

"There's someone asking for you at the front desk," Deidre' interrupted. "I think he's in a hurry."

Florence hurried to the front to find the young man that had helped load the water into her Jeep.

"Hello, Miss Florence. Nan sent me. And she sent these," he handed her a sack that appeared to hold clothing. "If you can, go put those on and Nan's waiting for you at Safe Haven."

In a complete state of surprise, she asked, "Am I supposed to know you?"

"Aww, come on, didn't she tell you? I am T.J., Nan's son." Laughing, he turned toward the door. "I gotta get out there, I left the snowmobile running and we do not want it to stop until we get back to Nan's. Hurry."

On the way to the room, she checked the bag. Heavy rubber boots with what appeared thick lining and a garment of insulated material; this could only mean one thing; she began to laugh, sounding like a crazy schoolgirl as she heard the door open at the front desk and a male voice calling Deidre's name. Even the sound of that male voice resounded all the way back to when she and Nancy Ann roamed the woods around Mosby. And now Nancy Ann had another surprise waiting, as if finding she had a son was not enough. Closing the door, she wondered for a moment why that male voice sound so familiar?

She returned, hoping no one paid attention; she had never felt so buffered before in all her life. She had pulled the coverall's with gallus's over her jeans, zipped up the matching jacket and started to the door when she realized there was more; a thick toboggan and gloves to match plus tinted safety type glasses. She gave the boots a once over and almost left them, but then they went with the outfit. If she could just slip out the door, unnoticed and unknown. She made a dash and was outside. There he was, her friend's son on a hoodless, track invention with one seat. She thought he smiled through a yellow tinted shield over his face, but the way his cap was pulled down to his eyes, she wasn't sure.

"Where do I sit?" He wrapped his left arm around his back, his gloved hand pointing down. "Behind you?" He nodded. She swung one leg across, trying not to touch him, but with that arm he moved her forward, snug against his body and she thought she heard him say, "hang on." Away they went, and she remembered later, thinking, there was no other mode of travel for the white banks of snow they crossed to Nancy Ann's house.

Chapter 3

Adam

He had a restless night and was up by four, going downstairs to work the stiffness out of his body from tossing and turning. The woman's laughter had tweaked a memory and last night sitting in the corner alone, at Joe's, he had watched her back up to the bar and study the sleet hitting the ground outside where Joe's restaurant sign had made patterns on the asphalt. He and Joe were lone souls these days. Catrin had left for New York, the day after Christmas. He wasn't certain the two of them were going to make it, Joe would give all to keep the family together since someone named Elizabeth had found his daughter, but Catrin…one never knew. Her parents were filthy rich and gave her more than any one person deserved. True, he was old enough to be Joe's father, well, almost. It was Joe's parents he had known. He was young then and they had mentored his life, regardless of the shamble his own parents made of it. He re-hashed his and Joe's conversation of last night.

"I was afraid you'd leave," Joe said.

"Well, I did. That lady, the one who came for water from the Inn, she was a brave soul to do that for the Inn. I suppose Galant left her again this winter to take his time in the sunshine. What island do you suppose he's on this year?"

Joe laughed. "Who knows? I always try to order enough supplies of items the Inn might need to take care of Deidre. Heaven knows Galant just goes off, scott-free. I assume he pays her enough for the trouble, but one day there will be a situation arise…" His words dropped off. "So what are we playing tonight? I will get the cards."

"Someone could take the Inn and make a nice landmark for Mosby."

"Why don't you do that? You have the means, you have just returned to Mosby and really with Elizabeth's fiancée from California bringing his business back to Mosby, I think it's going to grow."

"Elizabeth?"

"You said you remembered Nancy Ann, her mother. I only met her mother last week."

He finished the treadmill and went to the bars. Charlotte had hated the exercise room. Now it didn't matter if it had a sweaty smell for a while each morning. There were fresh air machines installed. He and Charlotte had lasted until they both could no longer stand each other and then she called the father of her child, changed the little girl's name, and left him and he was glad. By then her parent's had died, leaving her a fortune and Society knew nothing of her past and he for one, would never tell. He did miss the child but told himself she was much better off in the city than in the small village of Mosby.

He would become a distant memory, perhaps in some magical moment, one day, when she read from a book to her own children, she would remember, once there was a man who would sit for hours reading to her. These days, his social life was cards with Joe. Eventually, he would attend the church that held so many memories. He had to build up to that event.

By eight o'clock, he was hungry. He showered, slipped into a pair of jeans topped by a turtlenecked sweater and knowing no one could make it up the path to the house, he decided to go down and see how the Inn was holding up. Surely no one left in the night, and he was mostly interested in the white Jeep…and the women with the soft golden laughter that reminded him of a young girl with soft brown eyes and hair the color of cinnamon. He shook his head at the poetic reference. There was no hope.

He arrived to find the jeep still there and a few feet from it, a hooded person on a snowmobile. As he entered, he heard her laughter down the hall. He would have a cup of coffee, maybe a roll of some kind and wait. Surely, she would return within the hour.

"How's it going, Deidre?" She gave him a blurry eyed look and shook her head.

"It's like no man's land, Mr. Adam. Kind of like, every man for himself, if you know what I mean."

He poured his own coffee, took a seat and in less than fifteen minutes decided she was right. As he was rising to leave, he saw a person in full insulated clothing dash through the door and climb onto the snowmobile behind the young fellow from Joe's club. "Well, that's interesting," he said. "The young man I know, but who is that other fellow?"

"Not a fellow," a young man standing near, replied. "She just fixed this bandage on my wrist where I cut it. I like her."

"Then she has not a name, I suppose."

"Not that I know of," the young man replied.

Lonely, he left the Inn. There was little he could do on a day like this. He had wanted to make acquaintance with the Larson kid, all grown up now and coming home to Mosby to marry that girl he loved while a boy. His own story was not so different, except he had lost track of Fleur. They had promised, in parting from the motel, they would never divulge to anyone they had met one last time before he married Charlotte. He had no idea where she lived. They had kept their word.

Following the snowmobile tracks out to the end of the road, he was almost tempted to drive the direction of Safe Haven, but he was pushing the limit in the four-wheel drive truck, as it was, and he was uncertain how Nancy Ann would react to seeing him after all these years. How could she forget, he had left Fleur to face the sadness of their parting. Surely, she had told her best friend. He could not stand to see the truth on Nancy Ann's face. How could she not hold him accountable when she knew he and Fleur loved each other but he wed another?

* * * * *

Thomas James

All she could do was hang on. She had never been on a contraption like this. Her driver seemed hell-bent on showing her a good time. She thought she would contemplate Nancy Ann having a son she had no idea existed and for a minute she was a bit miffed, until her conscience kicked the left side of her brain and asked, what does Nancy Ann know of your son, only that you had a child and you never returned with him. The right side of her brain was silent.

She tried to say into his ear, "I thought we were going to see your mother." All he did was nod and then he was taking them up a steep incline. She wrapped her arms so tight around his waist her fingers knotted together in front, and she felt a buckle biting into her flesh through the gloves. Then, everything was serene, they were coasting along beside a line of trees that divided a field from a gulley with the usual markings of another man's land and then she saw it.

His parent's home. After all these years, she had not forgotten. On a weekend when he believed his parent's away, he had snuck her in to see where he lived. "Come up stairs with me, Fleur."

"I don't dare. If your parents come home, you know how they feel about me."

"It's not you, Fleur." He saw the sadness in her eyes. "It's their high expectations for me." He sit down beside her on the first step of the staircase that led to his parent's floor and on up to the three thousand feet of space they had given to him to do with as he pleased. How could they be that lenient in one thing but so tight minded on another? He placed an arm around her shoulder. "I would never hurt you, Fleur and if I am theirs, why would they?"

"Parents only want what is best for their child," she replied. "You are the only one they have."

His laugh was soft as the sadness in her eyes, "Well, I have not seen any siblings in the pictures you have shown to me of your life. Are there a couple of nasty little brothers peeping through the stair post at your house, or maybe two mean spirited sisters like Cinderella had to bear?" He lay a finger under her chin and turned her face to his. Kissing the tip of her nose, he wandered down to her lips. "I can't bear the thought that you might not come back to Mosby next year. What would I do?"

"You would find another girl to tell those sweet words and I would never know."

"I'll be playing varsity next year, is there any chance you will come, maybe during Thanksgiving break and can see me play?"

"My parents don't travel. Daddy says the holidays are his busiest time. I can only come for summer vacation."

Now his face was downcast. "The distance makes our lives so difficult. When I leave for college, I should have my own car. I will meet you, wherever you say. When you write, down in the left corner, always list a town and I'll look it up to see what you have in mind. I will know you have found a safe place."

"I do not understand why your parent's held you back from playing Varsity the last two years. Nan told me the coach wanted you when you were a freshman."

For a moment, anger surfaced toward his parents. "Mother was so afraid I would get hurt. My father saw that the teams had new uniforms, every year, and the latest equipment but his own son was not allowed to partake of all that finery."

She squeezed his hand. "There's nothing wrong with being loved that much."

"Do you love me, Fleur?" That haunted look was in his eye. It frightened her. "Sometimes I just want to hear you say it. I know they love me but theirs is a selfish love, almost as if they want to live life through me and that is not fair. They have more than anyone I know in Mosby, and they are not satisfied. I am supposed to be the fair-haired boy that accomplishes everything in their name and when I don't..."

She shook her head to clear the memories. It was still there, the grand house they built over Mosby. She wondered was his room still at the top of the staircase that spanned three levels. Lights were on, did they have someone always living there or had he and his Charlotte finally come back to see how the common folk live? Once he said, "I just want to be a regular person, Fleur, living with you that we might love and encourage each other and if we should have a child, I want that child to be just like you in case any of my parent's drive should flow through his veins." His, he said, not meaning it had to be a boy, only theirs.

"I am just a girl; I have no say over my life. I cannot promise you anything." Tears slid from the corners of her eyes, and he saw them.

"But you are. I see it and I feel it in my heart. Fleur, just love me for who I am, and I promise I'll make a way for us to be together."

They had sat for an hour, until Nancy Ann whistled, meaning her mother would worry if they were not coming down the path to Safe Haven by the time the sun started going down.

"Why can you not get out of this marriage to Charlotte?" She had asked the question, the last time she saw him. Their only night together. The night she became pregnant with the son he didn't know existed. He had held her so tightly she could hardly breathe as he cried, tears of a broken-hearted boy that had become a man long before he should have.

"I don't know, Fleur. I barely know her, but her parent's showed up unexpected that night. I was told to leave for an hour and when I returned it was settled, either I marry Charlotte or something terrible was going to happen to either one or both of my parents. "We've given you so much," they said, "this is the least you can do for us." His eyes had taken on a deranged look for that moment. "Sometimes I think there will come a day I will have wished I'd just let that happen."

She comforted him, that night, and the next morning they promised each other to try to live a good life despite what was happening and to never seek each other out, no matter what life brought.

She realized the noise of the machine had stopped. Nan's young man was standing alongside Nan and her new husband, and she was still sitting, no, straddling the machine as if she did not know they had arrived. "You can get off, now," the young man was saying as he offered her his hand.

"Where were you?" Nancy Ann was hugging her so tight she could hardly breathe. "You seemed to be lost."

"I was." She whispered into Nancy Ann's ear. "Your son that you forgot to tell me about took us on this long ride, through the fields above Mosby. Do you know who's home I saw?"

"Oh, my word," for a minute Nancy Ann was stunned. "He doesn't know,"

"Could we step away for a moment that I might regain composure?"

"Hey, guys, Fleur has something in her eye, we are going inside for a minute."

They hurried toward the back of the house. All she needed was to fall apart in Nan's arms. Deep breaths and short words got her though the worst part. When she had sobbed until Nancy Ann's shoulder was damp, she tried to control the uneven breathing that was becoming hard to produce. "I didn't know the knife would still twist in my heart," she said, replacing the tinted glasses to hide her eyes.

"I'm sorry." In sorrow, Nan glanced to where Jonathan and T.J. were examining one of the tracks to the machine. "I never imagined he would do that, I only told him to bring you here so we could play in the snow like kids again." She dabbed at her own eyes brimming with tears and then pulled a tissue from her pocket for Florence. "Here, we can't stand out here crying when we meant to make merry."

"No, we cannot." Florence quickly dabbed at the corner of her eyes and blew her nose. "So, what's next?"

"We will talk when we are alone, and I do want you to meet Elizabeth."

"Elizabeth? Your daughter?"

"Yes, she is hostess at the Club above the Inn." Nan laughed. "She even managed to pull T.J., into the working hours of the Club because the girls who are the waitress often can't travel the icy roads."

It was during a lunch break from being outdoors all morning and a need to warm up that Florence gleaned a bit more information concerning the current residents of Mosby. Nan said, "yes, Joe's parents lived up the hill and they built the club with their beautiful home to one side and mostly behind the club. Those my parent's age died off, of course Dad left us early in life."

"You may not know it, Nan," T.J. added, "But there is a new guy, as I understand his parents moved here when he was young. You probably knew him. Joe calls him Adam and he has never said the last name, so I just call him Mr. Adam, when I serve him. He seems like a lonely man, but I haven't heard the story. It's just that his loneliness makes me think maybe he doesn't have any family. Do you know him? From the past?"

"Who are you talking about, Thomas James?" Elizabeth came into the kitchen. "Sorry, I slept in. Last night at the club was a mess. First Joe's cook help didn't make it in and neither did the girls, but he," she pointed to her brother, "handled that quite well, if I do say so myself." She had completely missed seeing Florence and now that she was aware of a guest, stopped talking. "I'm sorry." She extended a hand, "I'm Elizabeth."

"Florence. Your mother and I were friends from an early age, cousins, too, as you may know."

"Why have we never met?" She gave her mother a puzzling glance. "I thought you were an open book?"

"I don't know," Nancy Ann replied, a mysterious sound to her voice, "Maybe we will release the silence of our secrets. Who knows?" She and Florence exchanged a glance, their eyebrows raised in conspiracy with no further words to the wise.

Elizabeth sit across from Jonathan. "How can you stand all the drama that comes with Mother?"

He reached for Nan's hand. "I love her. My life was very dull before she entered it."

Taking it all in, Florence asked, "Are you retired?"

"I'm beginning to wonder that very question," Jonathan replied. "It seems like as time goes by and Nancy Ann will become involved in her summer projects with her friends, Marge and Lettie...well..."

"You're thinking you may have too much time on your hands."

He smiled. "I am guessing you are facing the same." She nodded. "When we came," he said, "It was for a visit. Nan had turned the house over to Elizabeth, if I am understanding this correctly, but then Elizabeth and Derek renewed friendship, or was it love, Elizabeth?"

"Both," she grinned, "after a few duels of acting like we didn't like each other and…" she paused, "we did have to get Catrin out of the picture, for good."

Everyone laughed.

"So, when's the wedding?" All eyes were on Elizabeth.

"We thought Valentine's Day, but I don't know if we're going to make it and Derek is still working on moving his business back to Mosby." Her smile brightened, "and he insists we are building a new house."

"Will you start a family?"

"I don't think so, I'm thirties and that's a bit past prime to bring a little one into the world, don't you think?"

"Times have changed, women today have a career and then plan their family." Florence glanced Nan's way, "In our day, it was considered all right to begin early and have both at the same time."

"Mosby has its own set of rules," Nan agreed. "So, you and Derek can work that out."

"What about you, Miss Florence. Tell us how life has treated you." T.J., settled in the chair next to her. "We don't remember Nan telling us." He gave Nancy Ann a puzzled look. "Did you?"

"No, I did not and I'm not going to start that story now. Let's finish up and play a game."

"How about Scrabble?" T.J. grinned. "I have a feeling this lady can beat you."

No one could beat Nancy Ann, coming up with words they weren't sure were real words until T.J. found the old Thesaurus and proved himself wrong. "Anyway," he said, "Miss Florence, I think I better take you back to the Inn while there's day light."

"With the roads closed, maybe we can be together, again, tomorrow. I am so happy to have this time with you," Nan said, kissing her cheek. And the way their eyes met, Jonathan watching, knew there was a secret between them that possibly they would never share or, who knew? Maybe.

Florence climbed on behind T.J., this time feeling she had known him for years. She actually relaxed, and enjoyed the ride, that was until the shadows of evening turned their path into an unreadable landscape. She felt a jolt as the machine hit something solid and stopped. Tall blades of dry grass popped up on the right side and they found solid footing but on the left looking down the snow had pushed away to expose a pool of water beneath the cracked ice. Cautiously, Thomas James climbed off and reached for her hand. Once they were both staring down at the machine beneath their feet, he removed the shield to lean into her gaze, "We have it one of the old train track reserves. I am sorry Miss Florence, I sure wouldn't do this to anyone, but I'm going to climb up the bank and see if a truck might venture along here." He saw doubt cross her face. "You never know. It's about time for Joe's friend to make his way toward the Club. Those two play cards about every night, while Catrin is away."

Fate must know that young man, she was thinking as she saw him reach a high spot, she assumed the road they traveled that morning, and as though predestined, a silver truck stopped. T.J. turned to point down to where she stood. The man got out, walked to the back of the truck and together he and T.J. uncoiled a round of chain, hooked one end to the back bar of the truck and T.J. walked the chain down to where she stood. "Move back a ways, Miss Florence. I ask Mr. Adam to give it a good foot to the pedal to make this little darlin' move out of the embankment, because I am afraid just a little bit wouldn't do it."

She felt like joining him, when T.J. whooped as the machine reared up, gave a shake, and moved forward. He was standing riding like a hero. She could hear the motor catch and roar. Victory, she thought and her heart pound as though she was on the machine behind him, and then he was saying, "Miss Florence, Mr. Adam offered you a warm ride if you'd rather."

"Oh, no, Thomas James, you are my date for tonight, but please thank the nice gentleman for me." She tried to smile, thinking he could not see who she was in the evening's dusk, anyway, as she waved her hand. Thomas James walked the chain back up the incline, the two shook hands and the silver truck pulled away.

* * * * *

"Oh, Miss Florence," Deidre came to meet her. "I want to thank you for this morning. We've had such a day. Everyone jumped in to help and they all said how much they admired what you did this morning."

Bewildered, Florence asked, "What do you mean; what did I do?"

"Why, Miss Florence, you were the driving force for all of us. If you hadn't started helping me, why we'd still be trying to dump a bowl of gravy in that big old churn of a thing, and no one would have been happy and they'd probably flogged me."

Florence began to laugh. "Slow down, Deidre, your accent and my astonishment are about to overpower me, especially coming in here dressed like a welder's accomplice. I was afraid you were ready to tar and feather me but those are the sweetest compliments and please, if you will just thank those who might say something nice and let's forget it. Do you need help in the morning?"

Deidre was hesitant. "I just must play it by ear. If my answer was yes, it might be wrong."

"I rise early, I'll check with you, one thing though, do you have masks if I'm to help with the food?"

"Yes, Ma'am, back of the drawer where you found the packages of jelly."

Florence walked down the hall to her room. The parking lot had not been cleared. Alone, Deidre was mopping the breakfast room. There were several doors with trays sitting to one side for pick up. All in all, here was a situation that could easily get out of hand, if it wasn't all ready.

With a feeling of unease in her mind, she entered the card and waited for the green light of admittance to the room. When she had bathed and climbed into bed, her thoughts switched as if on automatic.

She guessed Thomas James to be about six feet tall, the man with the silver truck was taller and he called him Mr. Adam. Could it be Adam? If it was, Nancy Ann must not be aware of Adam's return to the community. Did her heart hope it wasn't him? She closed her eyes for sleep. And if it was, it would mess up her plans not to mention disrupt her world of finance.

She must put him out of her thoughts. He had Charlotte. She saw the hands of the clock point to each hour. When two o'clock arrived she found her cell, plugged it in to the charger and selected music, to help ease her body and possibly bring sleep. Chopin always soothed her nerves. He had lived a sad tumultuous life; in many ways she felt her life comparable. At five o'clock she dressed. She would go to the dining area and if Deidre was there, perhaps helping others would clear the cobwebs from her mind, and later if Thomas James came for her, she would find comfort in being with friends.

* * * * *

Chapter 4

He was restless, his mind wouldn't stop turning. He walked from one room to another, searching for some sense to life. Nothing seemed real. Why had he thought he could fill the void here, of all places in Mosby? Was It because his parents had lived in the big house, top of the hill? Questions, questions, questions, with no answer. The last five years he wondered what to do with the empty spot in his heart. The business was in good hands. He had worked hard and prospered, the resentment toward his parents faded as he found his own niche. He was good at numbers. It was his personal life they ruined. It was accepted by both families, he and Charlotte had nothing in common; they did not grow to love each other. He had been their pawn; his parents, hers, but the last five years, had he done any better? All he wanted now was to settle down, Mosby was as good a place as any, but he had forgotten how large, his parents' home, and now he was trying to make it his own.

He glanced at the clock. Two in the morning? He settled onto the sofa, plush and deep enough two people could sleep comfortably. Ridiculously, his mother had chosen it. Had his parent's ever snuggled as his little daughter called it, snuggling, cupped in warmth reading books while she was little and then Charlotte took her away and probably no one snuggled with her again. But she had made a place in his heart, Papa, she called him, as he read stories to her from a set of Golden books and then the exciting tales that came from his head that she liked best. The clock chimed on the half hour as he glanced at the picture hanging high over the fireplace with its gas log spewing flames that danced blue and red and reminded him of once sneaking Fleur into the house when his parents were away. But she had not sat on the sofa. No, from the staircase they had watched the flames that warmed the room. She would not venture farther. So, they had sat there and held hands as they talked about the future and his fear, she would not return the next year.

His eyes held to the picture over the fireplace; a garden with blooming flowers and a gate beyond to make one wonder did the world outside present itself as beautiful as inside the gate? Would the peace and calm go with the one who stepped outside? It was his gift, one Christmas to his mother to replace the stern-faced people of an old English setting that had hung there for years; knowing it brought no joy, opened no doors to serenity and in fact was as cold as a hog hanging in a frozen locker. Why she had ever allowed the decorator's choice to put it there, in the first place, he'd never know. She seemed to smile with relief when she saw the warmth and beauty of the painting he'd brought.

In the last five years, with Charlotte leaving, if he'd managed to do anything right, perhaps it was in the change he'd brought to Chatham. The family name was still displayed at the end of the lane according to his father's plan when the house was built. Sometimes he wondered, for this day and time if that might appear pretentious to those driving by. "Your ancestors came from England," his father explained when he was a child, which meant little to him at the time, as he repeatedly asked for a baby brother and his request had gone unheeded. He was an only child. If he had even one cousin, it was unknown to him. Glancing once more to the picture, his mind had gone beyond the gate He smiled remembering; each piece of furniture replaced, down to the last chair, always with the question in mind, what would Fleur have chosen but he kept the sofa either because the little one had insist they snuggle there as he read, or that he wished one day Fleur to be by his side.

Had he made a mistake, in returning to Mosby? How many times would he ask that question. A man his age should have more sense, but where was he to go? The apartment in New York was cold and sterile like a doctor's office. He longed for warmth. He had not realized Nancy Ann was in the community until Joe explained the beautiful hostess, Lisbeth, was the daughter of his childhood friend. "We haven't stayed in touch," he explained, leaving out the part of why they had not and then his mind found its way to the woman with the gentle laughter playing havoc with memories of Fleur. Could that woman who came to Joe's for the water, that he followed to make sure she arrived back to the Inn, the one with the young man that helped load the cases of water, the woman on the snowmobile with him, could that be Fleur. His heart hurt when he thought he was that close to Fleur, and he didn't know what to do.

Somewhere between hearing the clock strike three and six o'clock he slept. Awakening, he realized he slept on the couch and wondered when he reached for the thick Afghan at the end and pulled it over his body. Now he shaved, thinking what to do next and wondering at his usually calm self that seemed unsettled with a need to leave the house. Would the roads be open for travel? There was only one way to find out. He past the brogans he normally wore and chose boots that pulled over the jeans and felt snug on his feet with their own thick lining and waterproof soles. They were but one of many gifts received from the companies he owned. "We make these," the one walking him through the plant, had said, "you must take a pair, in case anyone ask you the quality of our work, you will know."

Remembering brought a smile. It had been the same with the chain used to pull the young man's machine from the embankment; purchasing the truck, he had moved the heavy chain from the garage to the bed of the truck, "who knows," he had said, aloud, "I might help someone, one day, with this." And he had. Yesterday. This was a new day. He would by-pass the Inn and drive toward the city. Or would he? Hadn't he always thought fate played a hand in everyone's life, but ministers said, "it is God's work."

Gods work. He thought on that, not disrespectful, but more sincere, he believed than he had been in a long time. How did one move back into society, when away from it the last five years? The people of Mosby had not known of his return, but they were aware that someone was making changes at Chatham, that huge house atop the hill. Deidre's mother came to deliver his instructions when business demand his attention elsewhere. It was she that rode hard on the various services, down to the carrying away of debris during the months of change, the new roof, rails to the entrance steps, refreshing the bricks needing mortar, as the list of repairs grew shorter she was sworn to silence as to his coming and goings. As was her daughter that ran the Inn for Galant.

Months passed before he met Deidre, born late to her mother, Gabriel, a love child without a father, her own mother tricked by a rich man that had a family of his own, hidden away in another state and he with no intention of claiming another wife, nor daughter. Gabriel had the taste for Society, even if it was the dregs, while Deidre was a fair child with a heart of gold, so unlike either of her parents, he wondered from where came the good? Gabriel said, "you will work with me and do as I say or get another job." He overheard the conversation as Gabriel was tying a cord to the library drapes and had her cell on speaker. Deidre replied, "I will find a job elsewhere, Mother, you need not feel concern over me."

There was more but he chose to put it away. Months later when all was complete, and he aid Gabriel; he heard her fuming. "You know I must leave. This job is finished, I am booked for another. I won't worry if you are with me." To which Deidre replied, "I cramp your style mother and I do not desire the kind of trappings you need. Leave with your mind clear and nothing wrong on your conscience, I like this little village. It gives me a feeling I can put down roots and not have to worry who I am and by the grace of God I won't worry about the next meal. Besides, we know you do not worry about me, anyway."

Gabriel had not seen him as she walked past the doorway of the room where he stood. There was a terrible wrinkle on her brow that did not go with the green lace dress she wore that day, as though she were headed to a party, not a three-hour ride on a plane to her next booking. He saw the cab arrive. Gabriel climbed in; a smile of happiness plastered on her face for the workers leaving to see. At the same time, he became aware someone stepped to stand by his side, gazing out the window, too.

"I didn't realize you were here. Your mother often leaves her cell phone on speaker as she talks."

Deidre nodded, shaking her head, as if wondering about the days ahead, perhaps not for herself but for her mother. "She is pathetic and doesn't even know it," Deidre said. As the cab pulled away her eyes met his. "I know I'm not supposed to be here, Mr. Adam, but I wanted to tell my mother goodbye."

"She would have come by the Inn to tell you goodbye…"

"No, Sir, she wouldn't. It would shame her."

"Are you employed by the Inn?" He asked at that time. Galant, he knew, but not this girl.

"Yes, Sir," she turned from the window as the cab was now out of sight. "I've been there a while."

"So, you like, Mosby. How, did you become a part of this little village?"

She took a deep breath, whether missing her mother's presence or something else. "I'm allowed lodging through the Inn and if the other people can make it in, I have Sunday's off and several other days here and there to explore Mosby."

"Why would you want to stay in an obscure little village that offers very little compared to the larger cities you must have lived in?"

For a minute she closed her eyes, thinking. "I love the peace and quiet, the calmness of the people, and it would be a nice place for a family," she opened her eyes to stare at him, then. "There's just something about it, Mr. Adam. The calm, I guess. Why are you here?"

Remembering now, he had chuckled, "To find what you just explained as your reasons."

"Would you give me a tour of your home, Sir? Perhaps it would help me to understand what my mother does."

When she had seen every room and commented on the colors and fabrics, down to the accent pieces, she said, "I understand you chose everything, it was merely her job to see they were put to order."

He nodded. "What do you think?"

"I am just in awe, Mr. Adam. All these soft colors make me feel happy and safe." She was thoughtful. "When my mother told me, I thought it would look lady like, but she forgot to tell me you used black marble in different places to tie it all together and that just seems to ground it and make it a home to feel good in." She smiled. "It makes me feel you did this for someone special." He saw the same features as her mother but on Deidre' they were sweet and kind, on her mother, mean and hard.

"That's a nice compliment," he had replied, caught by the pureness he felt in the young woman. "You have beautiful eyes, young lady. I imagine many people tell you."

"Yes, Sir, people tell me that. I must have gotten them from my daddy's side, but I don't know him or his people. Mother's eyes are brown."

He locked the door and walked to the truck, the rubber boots sinking treads in the snow. He had to turn loose of the memories that had such a hold on him. It was time to make new memories but where? But enough of the thinking and remembering that his thoughts would always be held by images safely hidden in his mind of Fleur.

A fresh snow had happened in the night, not a lot he reckoned, but enough to cover the old. Surely, he thought, the main roads would be cleared by now, while the secondary would be left until last. Using landmarks with which he was familiar he made it to the crossroads, one led to the Interstate, the other to the Inn and there before him, was a delivery truck turned upside down, one of the back doors swinging open, inside boxes spilling out, white uniforms and bed linens, laid upon the snow, white on white, but it was the driver, he wondered about as he walked the perimeter and found him, a young man he guessed somewhere in his twenties, picking up boxes on the other side of the truck.

"Are you all right," he called to be met by a blank stare, and no reply. Obviously, the kid was in shock. He walked toward him. "Are you hurt?" The young man shook his head. Adam saw the blood dripping from the end of his hand. "Come, let me have a look at you." At first, he was hesitant, but then placing the last box inside the truck's open door he came forward.

"Come with me," Adam said. "I don't have what is needed to see to your problem, but at the Inn Deidre should have. Look at the end of your arm. You are cut it seems or there would not be blood streaming off the ends of your fingers." He saw the young man hold up the bleeding hand and study it as a foreign object which he knew nothing about, but common sense meant something to him; he turned back to return from behind the truck with a white towel wrapped around his hand all the way up to his elbow. Adam opened the door to the passenger side and went on around to his own. The young man was in the seat and managing to pull the truck door shut. "Good. I'll take you to Deidre, at the Inn. I suppose you know her?" The young man nodded. "Then you will let her help you. What's your name?"

"Bradley." Bradley leaned his head against the back of the seat and closed his eyes. "I thought I was going to die, when the truck started turning of its own accord and landed upside down in the ditch."

"Why did they send you out, knowing the roads are not fit for travel?"

Bradley ducked his head as if in shame. "They didn't I private contract, and I'm needing money."

"Do you have enough to get your truck back to working shape?"

"I don't have enough to call a wrecker, if that's what you mean."

Adam took it all into consideration. If Bradley made it this far, the Interstate was operable, the problem was getting to it. The truck on its side meant one of two things, either the snow was deep enough to cushion the impact or, if it wasn't the damage was on the driver's side. Either way it had to be pulled back onto the tires and that meant a wrecker, probably with a thousand-dollar fee attached to it.

They arrived at the Inn, he parked and got out, waiting for Bradley to join him. As usual the Inn was bustling. More active than he'd seen the last week. People were ready to move on. The news had spread that the Interstate was open again. He looked for Deidre and found her coming in from the side door, the mop pail in one hand, the other struggling with the door.

"Good Morning," she said, trying to appear cheerful, but missing it by a few marks. "You're early, Mr. Adam."

"I heard you patched up a teenager pretty good the other day and now one of your vendors has turned his truck over and hurt himself in so doing, Have you time to help him?" Already she was peeking around the corner to see who he meant.

"Oh, Bradley. It is all my fault. I should have known he would be the one to try helping me."

"How would he know you needed help?"

"We are friends. He called before the lines went down, to see if this storm had hurt our business. Only Bradley would understand we are at the end of the world." Worry lines creased her brow. "But I never intended he should try to reach us, he asked, if we had enough linens and I told him the help could not brave the roads. Oh, it is just like him…" but then she remembered, "You said he is hurt."

"I don't know, except blood was dripping from his fingers. A couple of days ago a teenager said you fixed him up with first aid to a cut and he was pleased."

"That wasn't me, it's one of our guests. I…I think she is still with us…if I dare ask…"

By this time, Bradley stepped to Adam's side. He stood with the towel, red from his blood, and grinning at Deidre who was trying to ignore the blood and punched his shoulder as she passed by, "You silly," said, scolding. "Haven't I told you to never put yourself at danger. Your life is more important than a bunch of sheets and towels."

"Ow." He act as though the punch to his shoulder was damaging. "Where are you going?"

She gave him a quick jerky stance, "To find someone to sew some sense into your head."

"You've done it now," Adam said, dryly. "What if she runs out the door…"

Bradley interrupted, "She won't. She is the best…but I do have a worry if someone comes upon my truck with those doors open, they will take the boxes of linens and those towels are expensive, too."

"You want me to go back down and stand guard?"

Relief shown on Bradley's face, followed by a downcast look. "I can't ask that of you."

"You didn't. I asked you." Adam pointed to an empty chair. "Have a seat there and I'll know I'm leaving you in good hands." He was out the door and, in his truck, when he saw Deidre hanging out the door and rolled down the window but all he caught was, "thank you, Mr. Adam." He waved a reply.

Bored with sitting watch to an overturned truck filled with linens he called the nearest wrecker service. "Who is this?" The voice became more respectful, "You know it's going to cost you money."

"Have I ever failed to pay?" He listened to the apology in the voice saying they weren't sure it was him. "Well, it is. Do you want the job or not?" To which he was assured they did but why would some snot-nosed kid put himself in danger to deliver on one of the worst roads in town? "When can I expect you?" Adam checked his watch and just like clockwork in an hour the wrecker appeared, L.J. Cooper and his heavy-set brother climbed down, took a few minutes to decide what action they'd take and then unfurled six heavy straps they managed to strap to the driver side of the truck bed. It took much longer to dig through the snow to find a place to secure the straps than the time to pull it back onto its wheels.

"Ain't that the doozy," L.J. said, with an elbow swiping the drips of his nose away. "A few dents but not much considerin'. Now, let's see if she runs." He climbed in the cab, pumped his foot up and down a few times on the accelerator and the engine sputtered to life. "Put that big chain on the front," he hollered to his brother, "and let's pull er out."

"Didn't take long, what do you mean twelve hundred dollars?" Adam act as though it would break the bank. "Last time I saw you, you were bragging about your fair price, six hundred, I believe you said for a serious run, like someone in a deep gulley."

"But right now's demanding times," L.J. replied. "We jumped you to the front, 'cause you got the money."

"I'll throw in an extra hundred if you drive it up to the Inn and park it on the back side."

"Deal," L.J. agreed, holding out his hand.

"Half now, the rest when it's done." L.J. gave him a look. "Take it or leave it."

Three hours later he walked into the Inn's lobby. He had met one truck on his way back. He found Bradley well-bandaged, sitting in the farthest corner, his head back, mouth open and snoring like a banshee. Deidre appeared, shaking her head, "He's a big baby. The lady gave him something, a sedative, she called it and he went right to sleep."

"It would be best if he waits til morning to leave. We're beginning to get a bit of a thaw. Probably all your people will be able to leave. Maybe you can get a little rest then. How are you really making it?" He produced the keys and hand to her.

"I think they'd be burying me if it hadn't been for the lady that helped me. Not only does she take care of cuts and bruises, she knows how to sweep, wipe up mess and I couldn't do breakfast without her."

"She sounds like a keeper. Should I tell her personally thanks for fixing whatever was wrong with Bradley?"

"Even if she was the kind to expect it, you probably met the truck she was riding in on your way up here. She just left." Deidre saw his disappointment. "I'll tell her, for you."

Chapter 5

They were in her father's old truck. It was ancient, until one looked under the hood, everything up to date. Well, mostly under the hood, the upholstery could stand a fix and Marge promised she'd help Lettie on that job.

"So, you know how-to drive-in weather like this?" Fleur stared at Nancy Ann. "My life is in your hands?" Nancy Ann giggled and gave her a raised eyebrow look. "I'm not complaining, it is what it is." They passed a truck on the side of the road, a wrecker setting it upright, a fat man and a thin one. "Hmm, Jack Sprat could eat no fat, his brother could eat no lean. There's the understanding of the rhyme. What do you think?"

"I get it. One is fat, the other skinny. They're not local boys they come from the city. Why that sudden change in your expression?"

"I don't know, that other truck…I believe belongs to the man who followed me down the hill when I went for water for the Inn, my first night."

"You what?"

"Yeah, I did. Mr. Grumpy was grumpin', the Inn had no bottled water and the Club did, so I went. That truck followed me back and stopped to see I got inside the Inn, without falling. I don't know why, I felt his presence."

"You can say his name after all these years. You felt it was Adam. Why was that?"

"I don't know. Maybe because while I was at the club, there was this man in the corner." She paused, "I know you are thinking I'm hallucinating but that's not true, I've not had this feeling in years."

"Next time stop whatever you are doing and face it head on, that way you will know."

"It would be awkward, Nan. You know it would and if I did and he ignored me or flipped me off, I would be so humiliated, not to mention sad."

"Whoa," Nan gave her a troubled glance. "Is that the same guy that followed you down the hill and stopped and waited until you were inside? He doesn't sound like one to humiliate if you ask me."

"I wouldn't know if he has changed or not. We agreed not to speak or search for each other. He was always cautious and caring of other peoples need. I think that's one reason I was drawn to him."

"Not to mention he was drop dead gorgeous and being filthy rich didn't hurt a thing. But he wasn't my type, I chose from a page that reads as follows. He will love you until mid-life crisis hits and then he will look for a lover the age of his daughter. Goodbye you. That's my story."

"That sounds harsh."

"It was. Hurtful, too. Would you have believed Frank would be unfaithful?" They were silent for a while until Nancy Ann asked, "Why are you thinking about Adam? Have you seen him?"

"I don't know why he's on my mind. Was it him with your son. No one explains anything to you here in Mosby. It hasn't changed since the rare times I lived here, except some of our dear friends left here." They were on the Interstate now. "May I ask, where are we going?"

"I need some supplies at that craft store on the city square. Any place you'd like to visit?"

"I'm with you. You know, I hear they are already putting out Christmas items. But what do I need? I'm like a bird that's left its cage and don't know what to do. I had a feeling to return to the happy place of my youth and here I am with you and you have left your Jonathan home alone. Was there any problem leaving your husband behind?"

"Nope. He had plans. Bobby called from the church and said he needed to get a handle on this coming Sunday's scripture, could he discuss it with him. Jonatha was practically chomping at the bit. I just hope they don't mess up the kitchen too much. You know what I mean."

Fleur was laughing. "Nan, you love that guy. I'm so happy for you and a son, Frank's or…."

"I didn't birth that child, Fleur. Frank had an affair and thought he had to marry the girl."

"Just tell me the story. I don't think I could take in my husband's child from an affair. Mercy."

Nan finished telling her the gory details as they pulled into the craft store lot. Walking in a young lady called to them. "Hey, you two beauties, come over here and let me show you what you've been missing."

Laughing, and embarrassed, Nancy Ann bowed to the one who spoke the words while Fleur glanced around, certain she meant someone else and the sound of Nan's laughter carried down each aisle and people popped up and out from where ever they were and came to watch what would happen next. A pretty young girl wearing a smock that barely covered the short shorts, whisked a cloth over each of the women's shoulders, the two that were not hard to look at all, as she bid them sit while she performed magic, "not that you need it," she said, "But what's a bit of free beauty added where it can only make the angels in heaven sing and the poor mortals here below wish it was them?" She did a little dance for those watching. "Oh, yes, me darlins' I have the brogue of the Irish and the beauty in these finger tips to make these two walk down the aisle and you will swear, yes swear they are the highest in the land, the beauties you read about, the one's you wish would enter your gate. Now, my lovelies, hold your breath and I will treat you to the magic you long for."

Girls? Beautiful? That did it, they settled in the seat and let her work her magic. "Now, look in the mirror. Aren't you beautiful?" A group of ladies had formed around them and were all clapping. "That's for you," their person said.

They were on the way home when Fleur asked, "Did you get what you came for?"

"Yes, I think so, I was so mesmerized by the fairy godmother person back there, I'm not really sure." She leaned close to the steering wheel and turned her head to give Fleur a thorough going over. "The voice was yours but I'm still awe-struck at the beauty riding along with me in Pop's old truck. My dear, you need a throne, a crown and a scepter."

Fleur bent down to pick up a hammer laying at her feet and held it firmly in her hand, raising it as high as she could. "Will this do, fair maiden? I fear it is all I could find and we have to be careful it might turn into a frog and while you don't need one, I do."

"I promise, I'll see what I can do."

Nancy Ann took the back road in, that led up to the kitchen door. "I can unload these supplies and not have to drag them through the whole house. How about a cup of coffee and go to join Jonathan? I'm sure Bobby has left by now and Jonathan will love the company."

"Just so you get me back to the Inn before the wolves start howling at the moon."

"Wolves, huh? Is that the two- or- four-legged kind?"

Fleur laughed. "Take your pick. How does Jonathan take his coffee, black or with crème?"

"Different on given days, just make it and find some cups and there's a tray by the microwave."

Within minutes they were trailing through house, Fleur in the lead as Nancy Ann followed with the hot coffee and a plate of cookies. "Shouldn't we be sitting the table for a meal instead of snacking?"

"Depends on your husband, doesn't it? We had that wonderful bread and soup at the Bread House. Wasn't that delicious. I thought I'd died and gone to heaven." She pushed through Elizabeth's version of a café door, into the sitting room where Jonathan sit across from the fire, his feet on the hearth as he and another man's voice joined in a low rumble of laughter, and then a chair moved and there was silence.

"I guess Billy is still here," Nan whispered. She shrugged her shoulders. "Did you bring extra cups?"

"I did," Fleur replied, waiting for Nan to pull a small table to the middle of the four chairs. "That is ideal, chairs in front of a fireplace on a day the weather wants to beat you to death."

"But we didn't like it, did we?"

"Well, Jonathan, she hasn't lost it. She drove that old truck, just like when she was a teen, for all it's worth."

"The insurance rate won't go up, will it, then?" He smiled as Nan stooped to kiss his cheek. "I missed you," he said. "You, too, Fleur." He made a hasty glance toward the hall that led to the bathroom. "Umm, honey, I need to prepare you, we have an unexpected guest, you, too, Fleur. I hope you don't mind." The bathroom door opened down the hall as the women settled into chairs and footsteps came toward them.

"Her old truck is quite a master piece, isn't it?" The question was followed by a chuckle.

The look on Fleur's face, oh, my Heavenly Father, Nan was thinking. Jonathan said a silent prayer. Adam stopped in his tracks as he came into the room. She was beautiful. Jonathan had explained Nan's absence, "she and a friend have gone into the city in Nan's father's old truck. Would you believe, she's had everything under the hood replaced. It's all new. I believe she said all she likes is the upholstery."

What else could he do? Adam stepped to where Fleur was standing, undecided as to what he should do. He held out his hand. "Fleur? It's good to see you after all these years."

His hand held the aftermath of being washed and dried well, when she finally lay her own in his.

"Adam." He still wore that same fragrance. She hadn't forgotten. She pulled her hand back.

"I understand you and Nan were school mates, am I correct," Jonathan was saying. He didn't have a clue why Fleur's tan had receded. If she wasn't a class mate, then it shouldn't matter, should it? But when he started to ask, "Fleur, was the shopping spree up to par?" Nan shook her head in a violent way behind the two standing's backs. "I guess it was," he said, lamely, "but I don't see any packages."

Nan gave a nervous laugh. "They're in the kitchen. We came in the back way, as I had a few things to unload. Have a seat, you two." She reached across, where the dominoes were half hidden by Jonathan's long legs. "Here you go, Babe, sit the coffee and the cookies on the lamp table and we can use this one to lay out the dominoes." She had two piles ready in a moment's time. "How many shall we start out with?" She looked to the men. "We have a double set of twelves, I think five's the rule, but since it's double, how about seven each. That's a perfect number, isn't it? We lay down our number and the one with the highest goes first."

"That would be me, wouldn't it?" Fleur's voice was quiet and the others quieter. Something was happening and Jonathan couldn't figure out what it was. Fleur placed a double six in center of the table.

Jonathan laid a blank on one end, six on the other mid-way of the double. Nan held a six-one. Poor Adam, drew from the pile three times until the last presented a six-three.

"True to form, he wins. That's fifteen for you, my friend." Nan began to laugh, the laugh that always made others join in, whether they knew why she was laughing, or not. "You dummies, didn't even notice, I hooked my six one on to the twelve, exactly where I wasn't supposed to, but it looked all right to Adam, he got a fifteen out of it." Tears were in her eyes, the rest still laughing. "I can't believe you didn't catch it."

"So do we finish the game or talk?" Jonathan, was still a bit bewildered; he didn't know what was going on.

"I'd like to know your husband's life work, Nancy Ann, and whether he's retired or just on vacation and where Fleur's been all these years." Adam's interest in others remained true to the Adam Nan and Fleur had known those years past and Jonathan was always interested in people.

"I'll go first," Jonathan said. "When I was eighteen, I left for Oberlin college in Ohio, all I wanted was to have fun and hopefully gain a degree while I was there. It was co-educational and had a wonderful music program, which at that time I fancied a career in music, thinking if I was good enough perhaps being head of a church as their music leader, but I was just inexperienced enough in the ways of the world that I didn't understand too much fun might mean I wouldn't make that last statement come true."

"Don't stop there, tell us where the first stop after college took you, and fill in the years up to now." Adam leaned forward, genuinely interested, just as he always loved hearing about people's lives. Nan and Fleur made secret glances each other's way. Nan saw that Fleur was still sitting tall which meant she couldn't relax, and she was probably miserable.

"Long story short, about two years ago, I spent my first winter in Florida and attend a church service where I heard this fascinating good-looking man speak, and I fell for him. Sometime later, I ask a lady who usually sit by me, "where is his wife?" I wanted to lay eyes on a woman that captured this hunk."

"Nan." Jonathan was blushing as he pleaded with his eyes. "Don't say another word. Please. It's your turn."

"Me?" She grinned. "Well, before I married the widowed hunk, I was a mess. My first husband who I thought set the stars in the sky, you know, a lawyer hired to help Jesus, but I found out he was having an affair, his secretary, an orphan with no family became his child bride. She was pregnant, he left me. She had the baby and died two years later and I never ever wished that on her or him. Frank brought the kid home after I made my way to his apartment and met the child. We fell in love with each other. Without knowing my name, he called me Nan, for Nana. I finished raising him and he, myself and Elizabeth loved each other, and now we love the hunk with all our hearts." She turned to Fleur. "Your turn."

Fleur was studying the watch on her wrist. "I hate to break up a good party, but do you realize it is past eleven? Elizabeth and T.J. will be home wondering about us staying up past our bedtime." She smiled. "Nan, I hate to impose, but do you think that wonder in the garage could make one more trip, today, rather tonight?"

Laughing, Nan was up and headed toward the kitchen. "I'll get our coats. Say your goodbyes and follow me, remember, the truck's out back." But Fleur didn't follow. There was a delay. Nan returned to where the three stood, awkwardly silent.

"I would love the pleasure of driving Fleur to the Inn, if that meets everyone's approval," Adam was saying. "I promise not to make any wrong turns into the ditch, or turn over the truck as one young man did this morning and some marvelous woman patched him up."

"That would be Fleur," Nan said, nodding, her glance going to Johathan. "I didn't get to tell you, honey."

"Why, Fleur," Jonathan replied. "That's wonderful. Does that have anything to do with your career?"

When Fleur remained quiet, Nancy Ann said, "That's part of it. She can tell it all, when we play tomorrow night." She hand over Fleur's coat. Adam had retrieved his, and the two stood there, hesitant and expectant if that word could be used. "What, may I ask has happened? The cat got your tongues?" Jonathan cleared his throat. Fleur stared at the floor after noticing Adam's head was tilted to one side as she remembered he did when he was thinking. Finally, he explained.

"I asked, why should Nancy Ann get out in this weather when I'm driving right past the Inn. I ask Fleur if I might drive her back and she said a bit reluctantly, she supposed so, if you don't mind. Do you mind?"

"Truth, be, I'm hurt, but seeing as she is jumping up and down with joy and you have been a gentleman and asked, I suppose I'll forfeit my right. Drive safe and deliver my forever friend to the door." She buttoned Fleur into her coat. Kissed her cheek and then Kissed Adam's cheek, and led them to the door. "Don't forget, tomorrow night, five for dinner and later we finish dominoes and stories."

"Nan, I can't tomorrow night," Florence said, seeing her friend's disappointment, "Maybe skip a night?"

"Same ole Nancy Ann," Adam remarked, as he shook Jonathan's hand. "You are a lucky man."

"Yes, I love her very much. She has made my world a happy place, again." His smile beamed Nan's way. "I'm glad to meet you, Adam. I'll look forward to our next game night." Surprising even Fleur, he then turned to her, leaned across and whispered in her ear, that she alone could hear. "I went through miserable moments, too, and then one day a miserable moment turned into a happier explanation of life. If for nothing else, we must allow ourselves the explanation." He gave her a gentleman's hug and opened the door, stepping outside to let them pass through

"Brrr," he said, closing the door behind as he faced Nancy Ann right in front of his path to the fireplace. "No words, my love, just a prayer that His will be done, not anything we might do."

She waited, but he went in and set down, placing his feet on the hearth. "A good evening," he said, ignoring his wife's pout. When she reluctantly came to the sofa, he pulled her on to his lap. "Wasn't it?" She lay her head on his shoulder and her arms stole around his neck. He placed a finger under her chin, placing her just so, kissing her until she forgot what it was she wanted to know.

Chapter 6

"Fleur." He said her name, gentle and quiet, the way she had remembered all these years, but now that she was hearing it exactly as she had thought, strangely, she felt a stir of resentment flood her body until her face felt warm and she wished to roll down the window. "Fleur. Please, look at me."

She stared straight ahead. "For some odd reason, Adam, I find I cannot. I don't know why; it just seems that I shouldn't, but you may tell me what it is you wish to say."

"I don't have the words to say what has been on my heart, all these years that seemed longer than they actually number, but if I can see your face, your eyes, if you will look at me, I think you will see the pain I've borne and in time, I pray forgive me."

"Why would that be necessary, Adam. Haven't you lived a happy life?"

He started to reply, thought better of it and the words that almost slid out of his mouth turned into an almost sardonic laugh. Had he been a child, he would have cried in disappointment.

After a time, just as they turned the lane toward the Inn, he was able to say, "Do you remember the plans we had? How we always said Christmas would be such fun?" She ignored him. "We were going to celebrate holidays with such joy, because we were never allowed to be together those special holidays." Still, she kept her eyes straight ahead. He wasn't sure she was even listening. "Please, Fleur, may I pick you up tomorrow night? Or, whatever night you and Nan agree on?"

"I don't think that is appropriate." The truck came to a slow stop and before he could open the door and come around to her side, she slid from the seat and was already walking toward the Inn when she heard him calling to her. No doubt he would be standing in front of the truck for everyone to hear.

"I will be here at fifteen 'til five. I'll wait, if it takes until midnight for you to come out."

He knew her well and she, she knew he would wait, an embarrassment no one would perceive but she would know. Closing the door behind, she started down the hall to her room but she heard Deidre calling. "Ma'am?"

"Ma'am," Deidre drew closer. "I've waited for you. Bradley wanted me to thank you, Mr. Adam, too. Did he drop you off, just now? He paid for the wrecker fee to pull Bradley's truck from the ditch and isn't it amazing, not a thing was hurt after the truck was in that snowy ditch." She was becoming alarmed she had called on her guest, thinking they were known to each other but Ma'am wasn't replying. Nervous now, Deidre apologized, "Ma'am. I didn't mean to be nosey, it's just that he's a good man. I assumed you must know each other. I'm sorry…it's just these last five years he comes and goes always working on that house on the hill, never anything but kind and helpful. Sad, too, I believe."

Apologizing, Deidre finished, "I guess I thought you knew his story, how he was married but she ran off with her childhood boyfriend, they, who knew Mr. Adam, breathed a sigh of relief, when she divorced him. They said, "now perhaps he can find happiness." As if on second thought she added, "she did take their child. That must have hurt him terrible." Suddenly, Deidre's tone changed. "You don't feel good, do you. Go on to your room and you call me if you need anything, I'll bring it. You hear?"

Fleur nodded and hurried down the hall, once inside the room, she leaned against the door. Why should it hurt her to hear of his pain, hadn't she suffered? She shrugged out of her coat and fell across the bed, all she wanted to do was cry and she couldn't. So, the village thought the child his? That gave her no comfort, if anything it added to the anxiety she felt. Why had he returned to Mosby while she was here? Hadn't both he and Deidre explained he was working on his house. She was in such a perturbed state of mind, she wasn't aware the cell was ringing until she turned her head and saw it light up. Fumbling she found herself on the edge of the bed and answered in a breathless voice. "Hello."

"Mother?" She was so relieved it was Matthew, she laughed. "That's better," he said. "You had me worried there, for a minute. I was afraid you have not been taking your medicine. Have you?"

Startled, she had to think for a minute. "Yes, of course."

"Then why did you hesitate? You know what the doctor said. The problem will not be serious as long as you take the medication."

"Matthew Bennett, I think I'm old enough to understand what the doctor said, now why did you call?" His laughter was music to her ears and balm for her soul. "Is it that funny?" She felt better until she heard his reply.

"That little matter of business," he replied. It seemed she was not sure which matter he meant, "the one to do with Mosby."

Her voice became quieter, although she doubt anyone else was awake to listen in, at the hour. "Did you say, it went through?"

"Yes, didn't you want it to?" Now, he sounded perplexed. "When it caught your eye in that area newspaper, didn't you say it might be an answer to set you back down in the area you loved so much growing up? Haven't you found your cousin? Or, at least one of those women you met in those days, what was it, Leticia or Marcel?"

To back out now, her son would ask all kinds of questions. To ward off any suspicion, she replied, "The name was plain old Lettie and Marge." She did sound a bit stern in her own ears. "Mercy, Son."

"Now you are sounding more like yourself. Do I need to come check on you, or just write a check and see that the transition goes forward?" She heard the concern creeping back into his voice. "You won't get any nearer Mosby than that, will you?"

"No, I suppose not. Just write a check and I'll snoop around a bit, first."

"Snoop around, huh? Clandestine. Right? Doesn't that describe your new hobby?"

"I guess," she replied, a bit of moping apparent to her son on the other phone in New York.

"I'll catch a flight one weekend and pop in to meet all your friends, besides, I miss you."

"I miss you, too, if you'd find a nice girl to marry you wouldn't be missing your mother; just don't give me away, please."

"Good night, Mother." As usual, he was laughing. "I promise to see you by Christmas."

"Good night, John Boy." Of course, his name was Matthew Bennett, and she prayed she never had to explain their little throw back on an old series she often watched that took her back a few years and she used to say to Matthew, "life is like that in Mosby," until they reached a point he said it with her.

What had she done, gotten herself into a situation she couldn't share with anyone? Now that Adam had returned to Mosby, perhaps, she should go back to Nancy Ann's tomorrow night and test the waters. Heaven forbid, Matthew Bennett would make a stop in Mosby one weekend. Only Nancy Ann would understand his middle name being Bennett, but now how did she broach the subject to explain to her friend, not to let the question come up if she had children and what were their names? Oh, she pulled the cover from the foot of the bed, all the way up to her ears when she realized she still had her boots on and she had walked through the snow and down the hall. She was out of her mind and for good reason. For whatever endearing mood she had been in, naming her new born son, Bennett, now it seemed she would reap what she had sown. At least she had tucked the name in the middle and possibly made it a little harder for the good people of Mosby to decipher. Matthew said he would see her by Christmas, she couldn't wait.

* * * * *

Adam watched her walk inside. Her shoulders were as straight lined as he remembered her mouth was the whole evening. It all began the moment she realized his presence and last until she left the truck. He felt sad. Something he hoped for all these years had gone wrong, If, ever he saw her again there would be harmony, yet, nothing pleasant happened; he was left with the deepest feeling of remorse. He tried going to bed. If he was asleep, he wouldn't review re-runs of their time with Nan and her new husband. The clock struck each merciless hour and when it sounded the last note of midnight, he left the bed, wandered into his office and sit down in the chair in front of the computer. When the idea came to mind, he wondered how did one track a person through internet and was it really an invasion of privacy?

He typed in her name, as he had known it, Florence Ann Stokely. He ran through a dozen or more names and not one rang a bell. He did find a Matthew Bennett, related to a Florence Ann Stokely of Bennett Springs, Missouri and smiled, there was no Matthew Bennett in the life of the Florence he knew, especially in their last year together. He tried countless ways he might find the information he wanted. There was no mention of Florence Ann's career after graduating college. That was unusual. He tried the Nurse's web. A waste of time, he finally closed the program and wandered into the kitchen.

Suddenly, he felt he must get out of the house, in order to lose the darkness that surround his mind. He dressed in the camouflage-colored clothes he often used to hunt, picked up the ax and rope bought for a project now ignored and perhaps unnecessary to repair as needed for the one it was intended to please for she chose to have nothing to do with him.

There was a fog on the mountain, but he trudged on, sensing the cooler air. He was almost to the land above the Inn when he found the bridge made of rope. Most of the planks were missing and the rope had deteriorated to the point it was nothing but frayed ends. Now it seemed he must do away with the nonsensical object before a child tried transporting across from one piece of land to another. The fact he, Florence and Nancy Ann succeeded in building it was a test of their skill and lack of maturity, for in those days they were young. He began hacking away at the huge knots around a tree the girth of his waist, realizing the axe was dull. Foolishly, he remembered it was only a bit more than a sapling that bent in the wind the day they wound the rope around, tied it securely and knotted the ends, not to loosen, no matter how another tried. In dismay and ashamed of his own ignorance he kept on hacking away, stopping twice to sniff the air. Was the air getting cold as the wind began to stir?

He had only the first strand chopped loose, when he thought he heard a gasp as someone taken by surprise might sound and then as he listened, the awful thud of an object hitting where they determined the drop into the gulley was dangerous and they must not catch their foot to stumble unsuspecting to the depth below. The wind was picking up as he listened, playing tricks on his ears, the sound of a woman's painful cry, or a child. Of course, he thought instantly of Florence, but she would not climb the hill, nor come to the spot full of their memories, if she would not even speak to him or call his name the day before? He listened. Silence. His unrest heightened, was he hearing things that were not there.

In his mind, he saw her again, yesterday; she had aged more beautiful than he could have imagined, while remembering the pureness of her features as a girl, strong enough he visited that secret spot to see her laughing in the wind, closing her eyes to hide the pleasure she found being with him and then that one night they had together, the soft voice comforting him in his agony of parting, no promises between them, only goodbye, but yesterday, her beauty as a woman had presented an additional surprise within, that he felt the pain, again, of losing her.

Shaking his head to clear it of the endless barrage that hammered day and night, he turned back. He could not finish the ropes with the dull edged axe. He would return when the wind ceased it's in land blowing. Almost his stepping away covered the surety of a voice or a yelp of pain. He stopped. Could it be, someone was there? He thought of the boy at the Inn, a strapping young man that would invite adventure and the bridge might appear sturdy from the other side. Ahead, he remembered, if one watched carefully, there was a narrow path of dirt covered rock, they had not even told Nancy Ann existed. There it was again, almost a sigh of giving up, perhaps an animal, but he must find the spot.

Even now the narrow ledge he presumed to still be covered with dirt, held little snow as the wind lashed a spray of icy water over it and the rocks were slick beneath the soles of his boots. There was nothing to hold to, only his ability to balance the crossing and breathe a sigh of relief he did not fall. He turned, facing North, if he could find the bridge; now that snow was whipping up to his face, his eyelashes felt heavy as if they were freezing and he knew staying there endangered his own life. In five minutes, the weather had made a complete change but he must be certain it was an animal and not the boy, before he turned back to leave the mountainous terrain.

He stumbled just as he reached the rope, grabbing air to find someone had driven a stake to strengthen the bridges rope beginning and when he glanced down, there lay a boot, not one would easily discard but a good boot. Shielding his eyes he tried to see if anyone lay nearby when from the corner of his eye, he saw the body below, possibly of the boy wearing a red knitted cap with the insignia of a prized team, one gloved hand beneath the twist of the body the other across his chest. His heart did a jump as sweat broke on his brow, if he could safely reach him, he would have to rely on the strength of the rope in his back pocket to help pull them both back up to the top of the bank.

There was not a tree to tie the rope around. He tried the stake, wondering if it would hold, to find it had been recently driven into the ground, possibly even this day before the storm arrived. He had no choice, but to knot one end of the rope to the stake, the other around his waist to help him make descent to where the boy lay. His two hundred pounds plus a guess the boy weighed possibly thirty over a hundred because he was tall and lanky, would push the strength limit of the rope. He made it down, a foot at a time, praying the rope wouldn't break or the stake pull free of the ground. He saw the mask over the boy's face had pushed to one side and pulled it back in place. Sliding an arm under the boy's waist he prayed his body would conform to his own and not dangle stiffly causing an imbalance. He had wound the rope around one gloved hand and now with the other arm beneath the boy tried to rise enough to dig one booted foot into the side of the embankment.

Just when he thought they were going to make it, he felt the rope lengthening, dropping into a loop that didn't allow him to pull, but to give the sense they would plunge to the bottom, past where he found the boy, to gain speed and hit thirty feet below. Frantic, now, he pushed the boy's body up, needing something to rest his foot on in order to shove him onto the upper ground; searching in what seemed forever, he found a rock that extend out and raised his foot carefully to claim it, taking a deep breath with his hands a cradle to the body and the boy was there, with one last burst of strength he hauled himself across the boy, momentarily using every ounce of will he possessed not to hurt him, as his fingers dug into mud, pushed deep and he was laying with the wind whipping around them, the air freezing the sweat on his brow and he wanted to cry for what he was given, knowing where the strength came from, for he did not possess it on his own. Finally, he managed to stoop, and removed one glove to place a finger against the side of his neck. There was no pulse, nothing. He removed the mask. The boy's lips were blue. He leaned down but felt nothing on his cheek. He had no choice. Adam began chest compressions, counting, was it twenty or thirty? He chose thirty, firm compressions followed by two breaths, was it two? He could manage two. He was about to give up, when he felt something, maybe a flicker of an eyelash against his cheek, a movement so slight of the body, a difference the shape of the mouth, he didn't know, but he knew something changed and he had to get help.

Where was his cell? No doubt he lost it, or had forgotten to bring it. He didn't know. He was in a mood when he left the house. His finger was so cold he could barely find a pulse, but there was a slight movement beneath his finger tip. He didn't know whether to continue the chest compression or not. On gut instinct he made his body rise, got his bearings and raised the boy to his left shoulder, wondering if he dared tie the rope around them again or take the chance it would be better to leave the rope behind and try to get back to the house.

He chose the latter, tense to the point of shallow breaths, he knew he had to get hold of himself. Ever watchful of the path ahead, he put his foot down, careful each step and found he must also watch for low hanging branches bare of leaves that might catch the boy's face or worse cause him to drop him from his shoulder. One yard became two and finally a mile.

He fumbled to open the door, and stepping inside, saw his phone lying on the island that divided the rooms from each other. He laid the boy on the first sofa in order to use the phone free handed. He found the walk had tired him, wishing he had but a moment to calm the stress of his body but his mind was fixed on calling for help. Quickly he dialed 9-1-1. It was almost comparable to praying, he thought, aware that his own body was nearing heat stroke. He unzipped the coveralls to the waist as a voice ask for information. "We have a relay station about fifteen minutes from your vicinity," the lady said. "We will see you soon. Can you send someone out to the road, to direct our arrival?"

"Send someone out to the road," he said, out loud, when it suddenly dawned on him, he must call the boy's father. He dialed Deidre. When no one picked up, he text, "Deidre, that young man that's staying with you. May I speak with his father." Within minutes Deidre text back.

"I'm sorry, Mr. Adam, both he and his son have left, first the father and then the son saying he was going for a walk and I have no signal, other than to text."

Alarmed that he had missed seeing the boy's father, he wondered was he below or near where he'd found his son; but first things first, the boy needed attention and that was what he was going to get. He tried to comfort his conscience; he would have seen a person as he gaged the distance. Hurriedly he checked the boy's pulse.

It seemed to be stronger. He rezipped the coveralls, glad he hadn't removed the cumbersome things and was ready to stand out by the road. He was limited in knowing what else to do, but if standing by the road would bring help, he could do that. He grabbed a flashlight and ran until his sides hurt. How much time had he used inside the house? He practically hugged the brick façade that held the family name and then the ambulance caught the flash lights beam and turned up the lane for him to follow. They were removing supplies he supposed they felt necessary, as he approached.

"We will need you to move your vehicle, Sir, that we might be closer, for transferring the patient to the ambulance," were their first words. He watched a man and a woman wearing white doctor coats going up the steps, as he panted for breath and tried to holler, "He is on the sofa, in the first room. His pulse is stronger." If they heard, they did not acknowledge. They were there. It was all right now. He could catch his breath.

* * * * *

By the time he maneuvered around the ambulance to return to the house, the man was stepping out the door, a puzzled expression on his face. "Sir, I'm wondering if we have made a mistake in answering the call…but you were standing by the road motioning us in."

"That's correct," Adam replied. "I gave your call center the address but they said I was to stand by the road."

"But, Sir," the man glanced toward the house, as if needing back up to what he was going to say. "That is not a boy. Did you tell us a boy was in need of medical attention?"

"I did." He was tired, sweating beneath the clothing, not because they were having a heat wave but he supposed the stress of carrying the boy on his shoulder through the woods. In all, now being questioned he felt a bit belligerent. "Do you not treat the male gender?"

"Sir, the patient is a lady. Can you not tell a difference." Apologetic, he added, "I grant you, at first glance we didn't know, with the mask and the cap over the ears, but if you will step inside, I believe you will understand what I am saying. And I might add, you should prepare yourself, the lady is not a, shall we say ..." He searched for words, "a happy camper?"

For what it was worth, if anyone cared, Adam hoped he didn't have a heat stroke. "I walked a good mile with that boy on my shoulders, barely breathing like a bag of sticks on my bones, don't tell me he is a woman and unhappy to boot." He took a deep breath and followed the medical guy into the house and there sit Florence, the red cap in her hand, her hair flowing on her shoulders, her face pale but her eyes snapping.

"How dare you?"

Adam was in shock. "Fleur?"

"Don't call me that." She turned to the lady that Adam assumed was a nurse. "My name, as I told you is Florence and this, this, this, man. Where did you find him?"

"Good. So, you two do know each other?" The woman was doing the questioning, the man had backed to the wall.

"Barely," Adam said, weakly.

"We used to," Florence replied, hotly. "Why am I here?"

"If we may recap what the call center told us, please." The woman held up a hand. "Mr. Adam, here, was checking a bridge up on the rise, and heard a moan and upon investigation found a male, er, female form passed out near unconscious, I believe it was." The patient seemed in denial, but the one recapping only paused. "He administered CPR for a length of time and when the pulse stabilized, he carried the person out of the woods to the home where he was able to call our center and he assured me he would be waiting at the end of the road to direct our path to the patient."

Speaking to Adam, she asked, "Was that about a mile through the woods?" Adam only nodded. "Well, it seems Miss Florence has regained control of the situation with her heart, stating that she forgot to take her medicine this morning, a generic, propranolol, I believe she stated and the cold atmosphere of the weather changing plus a higher altitude was severe to the point of losing consciousness." The woman was having a hard time controlling the humor she saw in the situation while her partner evidently had decided to see how this played out.

"Miss Florence. We suggest you remain for the next twenty-four hours if this gentleman accepts you as a guest and his agreeing to keep watch over you during that length of time or you can allow us to admit you to Stinger Hospital, first, a small silhouette care center, which is an extension of Mercy Stinger Hospital. It is about an hour's ride from here; once we arrive, they will decide if you are stable to spend the night there or we should continue on to Mercy Stinger, and we are ready to do as you wish." She peered into Florence face. "It is the law, Miss Florence, if we make a call we are not allowed to leave without our patient, unless that patient insists or agrees to remain where treated for the length of time, we deem necessary."

She reached an inner pocket of the white coat she was wearing to remove a small recorder. "I will need your last words before I take this instrument in for our call center to verify our medical treatment and parting advice to you, should you decide to accompany us to Mercy Stinger or remain in this gentleman's home." She was now looking to Adam for consent. "May we leave our patient in your care, if she should decide that is a wise decision or merely thank you for saving her life this day if she decides it is better that she accompany us to Mercy Stinger?"

Adam was as much in shock at this strange turn of events as Florence, but he saw her flinch at the words asking his consent. It was obvious she found it distasteful to stay in his home. He did his best to nod. "Yes, Miss Florence is welcome to stay. There's a guest room that she can use."

"Are you ready to make your decision, Miss Florence. If you decide to stay do you need my assistance in helping you to your room?"

Florence felt as if an ugly charade was playing out before her eyes and she was the victim. If she went with them, how would she return to the Inn. If she stayed, under the auspice of believing he had saved her life, indeed; then she had to be nice, didn't she and she didn't feel nice. She felt fate had decked her with a heavy hand and he held all the aces. She was furious inside, and with that fury her heart began to beat faster and faster and she knew if she didn't straighten up and behave, she would go out like a light.

"If I might sit here, quietly, my body will catch up with my mind and my heart will remain steady and everything will be all right." She noticed Adam had slumped on a tall stool at the huge island. His head was practically ready to lay on his arms like a child caught in a situation not knowing what had happened, why it happened and how he had become a part of it. No, she wasn't forgiving him, she just hadn't figured out yet where she was or how he found her. Walked a mile carrying her? Phew. He couldn't make it three feet carrying her.

"Would there be any chance you might have medicine in those coverups with all those zippered pockets?" The man asked, and she turned to study him as she tried to grasp the question. "You mentioned you had not taken the medicine today; we don't want this to happen again." The gear Nancy Ann had sent to her for the day of play on the snowmobile seemed to be her choice of wear today and there were plenty of pockets. That day she had put a small bottle of medicine in one of those upper pockets. Had she removed it that night?

She began to pat those upper pockets while everyone looked on. Finally, she felt a small lump, and pulled out the little brown bottle of pills. Everyone seemed relieved, except Adam, he was still sitting at the Island, his back to them and he didn't move. He didn't even turn around. The other two cheered.

The woman was examining the pills. "Phil, get a glass of water, please." She continued looking at the pills. "The pink is Propranolol, right?" Florence nodded. "Tylenol 3? You have trouble sleeping?" Another nod. "What's this?" Florence leaned forward and whispered. "Alright. We are all set for a couple of nights, if it takes that long. Are you all right with these meds?" Florence nodded. "All right, we will leave you at this time and Phil has brought the water, if you will please take the Propranolol. A Beta Blocker, right?" Florence was taking a sip of water and managed to nod. "Do you want me to help you to your room or waken Mr. Adam?"

"Wake him?" Florence couldn't believe he had gone to sleep. Her first thoughts were not the best, but by the time the two had left the room, out to the ambulance and she could hear them drive away, she felt a bit concerned. If it was true he had carried her on his shoulder a mile, that was questionable, a man his age carrying a woman, even a child, was a myth and she wondered why he would start such a story and she was taller than a child, if he did carry her that far, no wonder he was tired. She felt a bit of remorse, but pressed it down.

Now what was she to do? Hobble to the nearest room, find the bath because she had been trapped in dirt and rubble spewing in her face as the wind whipped around. It had been terrifying. How could she have been so foolish. But her thinking was if a child thought to cross to the other side, sometimes children had no fear. It had been her intention to close the bridge.

She tried to stand, whether from weakness in her body or effects of the medication, her legs buckled and she was on the floor. She couldn't use her legs but she must. Perhaps it was due to a complete shutdown of being ill and not rising up she found it hurt to do the regular normal things one must do. She knew all about that; was she seeing this situation, right? And yet her mind wandered. What was he doing in Mosby? She gripped the little bottle tighter in her hand, wondering why she had it.

Her mind was made up. She could handle this and she would. Practically on her belly using her feet to push off, elbows bent and hands to the floor, Florence moved one room to the next, while he's sleeping, she would tour the house. She found it was nothing as she suspected. The lay out was perfect. The furniture appeared new.

She could live in this house.

She tried standing again. With struggle and effort and the help of an end table she was standing. Now what? From here she heard a clock striking the hour and saw the sofa with a cover draped across one arm. She made her way to sit on one end. She must think this through. Years past when they thought they would marry he had said only one thing, that she decorate their home as she wanted and they spent many hours dreaming of the time *they would be together.*

Why had he used all the colors she loved? He married another. Had he never loved her? The house spoke of their time, not his Life. Something responded to her question as she glanced up, over the fireplace, A Peaceful Life stared into her world, and she almost lost it.

The year her parents allowed her to stay with her aunt and family an artist had come to the school to work with those interested in furthering their talent and he asked if she would be his model. When it was finished, the artist asked, "what shall we name it?"

"A Peaceful Life," came from the back, and their instructor asked. "Why that title? What do you see in her? She's just a woman working in a flower garden." They took a minute to consider the hours they'd tried to imitate what he showed them with the brushes. "She is happy, nothing hampers her smile," said one, and another, "no one seems to wish her harm." One by one the instructor listened as he walked about viewing their work. Another replied, "the smile is genuine, but there's mystery in the smile." Heads were nodding. Florence heard Billy say, "The smile suggest she hides secrets that makes her both happy and unhappy."

The discussion buzzed around, as they forgot she was the model and when all was said and done, she prayed they wouldn't remember when they walked out the door. But through the years she wondered who purchased the painting as it rest in a glass window, downtown, and then one day it was gone. Why was it here, over his fireplace. Adam. Adam? She sit up straight. Adam bought it? She glanced to where he sat humped over, his shoulders nearly touching the island surface, his arms were folded, his head sideways now and he was sound asleep. She wanted to pounce on him and ask what right he had to the painting. She tried to stand, dizzy, catching the arm of the sofa before she went down, rising again to take a step his direction until she stood looking down at him.

Then she saw the scratches on his cheeks, one diagonal from his forehead into his brow was crusted with dried blood and his fingernails were filled with dark dirt. Hadn't she heard Phil say to the woman, "he's not a young sport, Edie, maybe we should check him out. I am a lot younger than him and I couldn't carry a child out of the woods a mile without some assistance." In her mind she heard the reply. "Why wake him, Phil, he's resting, isn't he?"

She huffed out a breath of pure frustration. What was she to do? They said she needed to stay the twenty-four hours, preferably forty-eight, but they saw the resolution in her eye to defy all three of them. She was that angry, maybe with herself more than anyone. Now that she was up on her feet she wandered into the hall between the rooms that ran away from the large combined dining and sitting room with its fireplace and her picture, and found three bedrooms.

Quietly she opened the closet doors, finding the first one empty of clothing. In the hall she saw the linen closet and she could tell his room, heavy furniture, a four-poster bed, the posts massive and nearly touching the ceiling. It appeared to be new and reminded her of advertisements from the city's best stores. He was always neat. There were no surprises, other than she wondered why the rooms appeared freshly done and were as they had planned, but he and Charlotte had been married twenty years.

She was beginning to feel the weight of the medication. She moved into the third room. They had pulled her from the insulated clothing but that didn't mean she was clean. If she took a bath, what would she wear? She opened the doors to the closet and found a woman's silk robe, apparently unworn, a tag hung from the inner collar. Moving quietly about the room, she checked the contents of the tall chest with folding doors, finding it empty and moved on to the dresser with a bank of three long drawers to find three white boxes, similar to a gift box but without ribbon or tie of any sort adorning them, and under the lid white tissue paper.

She carried the three to the bed and sit beside them, opening first one and the next and then the last, to sit there staring. Who had he purchased lingerie for? Curious, she took in the surrounding furniture, the pale blue of the wall, the drapes with silk tassels, the quilted comforter with its matching throw. Her favorite color. How dare he?

Hastily, she pressed the lids back onto the boxes, stepped to the dresser and placed them inside the drawer, but her eye caught a sales slip and she was curious the date of sale. She read it and read it again. Within the year. So, he had a mistress or a lover because the closets were empty of Charlotte's clothes. She had seen one satin house coat. Angry, she chose one of the gowns, and not daring to look back hurried into the adjoining bathroom. She ignored the oval tub, stripping away the filth of her clothes, wadding her underwear in a ball and placed them and the little brown bottle under one of the bed pillows and stepped into the shower.

Finally, scrubbed clean, from head to toe, she dried her body, completely aware of the depth of thickness to the towels, the expense of the powder and the fragrance of the perfume she used. But the sporadic energy gave way as she sank onto the bed, barely giving her the strength to pull the sheet and light blanket to her chin as she closed her eyes, forsaking prayer, she had one one last mean thought; sadly to heap ashes on his head, except she went to sleep.

Chapter 7

Adam awoke, stiff and cold, the coveralls unzipped to his waist, the flannel shirt damp and drool crusted at the corner of his mouth. His sleep had been a nightmare, as though one eye open he waited for the next horrendous event, and then he realized, it was a nightmare. He tried to rise, the cumbersome clothing holding him back, his head in a stupor as he remembered it was real; he had carried the boy a mile through the woods only to find the boy was Florence; Florence sitting on his sofa in the great room as the decorator called it, with her snapping eyes full of malice, words popping out of her mouth with hatred that he had brought her to his home in order to call nine-one-one.

What was he to do? He had not realized the boy was Florence, nor yet understood why she was there, across the ravine, and had he not heard her moan and crossed that treacherous path of rocks, just wide enough for one foot to fit in front of the other, to find her, caught in the fall as she was, with the night growing colder, in danger of dying because few people would have remembered the trail, until too late. Worst of all, reluctantly she now sit on his very own sofa.

He turned so fast he almost fell; his feet caught in the coveralls to drop down, around his shoes. She wasn't there. They had taken her, no doubt lest she lose consciousness again. Whether it was relief or sadness that she was gone, he was not certain, but to escape the anger in her eyes gave him a moment's comfort. In all the times he had known her he had not experienced such agony to his soul as he had felt her contempt of him this day and hearing such bitterness.

All the working out to stay fit, the hours of weightlifting, had not prepared his body for the mile he carried her through the woods. Pure grit and determination had brought them to his home, the nearest place to make the call for help and after placing her safely inside he had returned to the end of the road to wave in the ambulance. The medical technicians had determined she had forgotten to take medicine that morning and the high altitude and changing temperature had caused her to pass out. No, it was more than that, for he had done his best with CPR, not that she would ever thank him.

Even if he called, they would not tell him her condition, he was not family. He sank onto the high-backed stool, placing his elbows on the island, his head in his hands. How had his life come to this? He had dreamed of the day he would find her and bring her back to Mosby to show her the home he had rebuilt as near to the dreams they shared in those days when they believed they would marry. But his parent's intervention had destroyed his life. He had no knowledge of what happened to Florence. They had promised that one night they spent together, never to contact each other again. And yet, some sixth sense had told him, as he sit in Joe's Club, thinking the woman who came up the hill from the inn for water reminded him of her, that he must not give up hope. As long as there was breath there was hope.

He had not eaten but he had not an ounce of energy left to find even cheese and crackers. Leaving the coveralls laying by the back door, he walked in darkness to his room, undressed and stepped into the shower hoping warm water would relieve the aching muscles in his arms and back but found himself standing there for the longest unable to make himself get out. Habit must have finally moved him from the shower and the bathroom to fall uncovered on the bed.

* * * * *

His dreams were clouded with failure, for not standing up to his parents, for letting Charlotte keep her lover, the father of her child, for letting the years pass until both of her parents were dead and only then was the curse lifted off of his own parents' name; a scandalous curse that would have put them in danger and made him the bitter root of his birth. He heard a man crying and awakened to find his cheeks damp with tears. He was drawn up in fetal position, the spread wrinkled beneath his body, not a sheet for cover. He arose, found pajamas against the cold, and returned to bed but could not sleep; rising again to dress and leave the house.

It was three in the morning. He would drive the hills until time for the Inn to open. Only then would he settle to have coffee under the compassionate eyes of Deidre. If he had a son, he would pray that son would find a woman to marry as kind and considerate as Deidre. They seldom touched on the private personal thoughts of each other, but seemed to recognize they were kindred spirits, some way fate or the goodness of the Lord allowed each to sense either a longing or sadness in the other. In another life they could have been father and daughter.

Fifteen minutes later he found himself circling the drive of Mercy Stinger's small affiliate to the larger hospital an hour away. He once read it was more or less a satellite station, for emergencies when weather did not permit travel over the mountainous roads. He recognized the ambulance, he had directed up the lane to his home, by its number. Not wishing to embarrass himself further, if the two were still on call, he called direct and ask if a lady named Florence had registered during the night and was promptly told there was not a patient by that name, perhaps his person was taken to the main hospital.

He turned back. It seemed the roads were open all directions, but with the weather report promising snow, he wondered if Deidre's guests would be leaving quickly after breakfast was served. The restless feeling was invading his nerves and he needed something besides coffee to take his mind off yesterday's happenings. At the Inn, Deidre was scurrying all directions trying to keep up with the traveler's demands. She gave him a weak smile and courteous as always said, "I'll get your coffee, Mr. Adam as soon as I check out Mr. and Mrs. Bobart."

It was obvious, all of her people had not arrived, and she was in serious need of help. He pondered whether he should offer, and finally ask, "Deidre, is there anything I might do to help out?"

"Mr. Adam, are you familiar with running credit cards and using a cash register? It's a rather old one, but still works."

"As a matter of fact, I believe I could do that."

Her relief was obvious. "Sir, I trust you completely, if you could help these folks check out, so they can get on the road, it would free me to see to the kitchen." He nodded. "Here's the list of names, and how many nights they have stayed and any incidentals they may have charged. Only a few will pay cash, most you will just have to run their credit card." She paused a minute, and then said, "I think that's it."

It was ten o'clock when the flow of guests leaving slowed and Deidre came from the kitchen. "Please, Mr. Adam, let us find a spot over by the window and have a cup of coffee. There's enough food on the hot plates for a dozen or so, if anyone else happens in at this hour for breakfast." She was carrying a family size pot of coffee and set it on one side of the table. Adam picked up two cups and followed.

"I can't thank you enough," she began. He reached across and patted her hand, before raising one finger to his lips as if to silence whatever else she intended to say.

"How are you holding up?" He asked. "You are looking a little pale. Maybe you need to eat something."

A blank stare went across her face. "I don't think I've eaten since yesterday morning. That's when we got such a scare. I didn't know Miss Florence had left early to see her friend, Miss Nancy Ann, down the road and I tell you we were all wondering where she was."

It was his time to wear the blank stare as he waited for Deidre to continue. "She was missing?"

Deidre took a deep breath, "We thought so, but the young man she bandaged up when he cut his hand, said he met her going out the door and she said she was going out to reunite with old friends."

He needed a moment to consider this piece of news. Obviously, something was misconstrued in the wording of the young man, but then again, it was like Florence to waylay any type of information that spoke of her personally and if she was going up on the mountain, evidently, she didn't wish to explain why. He nodded. Yes, that was Florence, by reuniting he wondered, could she possibly mean old memories? He would leave her secrecy intact, knowing she was at Mercy Stinger being treated.

"I tell you what," he said, instead, "why don't you sit here a minute and catch your breath and I will fix us a plate of breakfast, just whatever is available. Would you let me do that?"

Her eyes brimmed with tears, but she quickly put her hands to her forehead to hide them. "Oh, Mr. Adam, I can't…" but he was already moving toward the kitchen. The girl was worn to the bone, that much was obvious and still had the rooms to clean by herself. He shook his head; he wouldn't be much help there. Right now, he was placing a spoon of scrambled eggs, bacon on one plate, sausage the other and gravy on a second biscuit. He guessed they had earned their meal and he hoped she would eat.

He noticed the pale look of her skin was being replaced by a healthy pink glow and thought all was going well until she got up in a rush and headed for the rest room in a mad dash. He was finished eating by the time she returned, apologizing. "Think nothing of it," he replied to her apparent discomfort in the necessary apology. "That happens when you miss meals and then try to compensate."

She wore embarrassment like a hair shirt, there was no missing it. "Thank you, Sir," she mumbled. "I need to get to the changing of sheets and start the laundry."

"The roads are open, won't your service run and save you at least one job, having to do laundry?"

"No, Sir, there's been a bad accident on the highway and traffic coming our way has been blocked."

"Misery does love comfort, doesn't it? I wonder if that's like death and trouble, it comes in threes?"

Deidre gave him an odd glance as she clutched her stomach and took off running again. He was almost relieved to see the young man with the bandaged hand coming through the door. "Say, there?" He motioned and the boy came over to see if there was something he needed. "It's Terence, isn't it, your name?"

Puzzled, the boy was waiting for him to get to the reason for calling him over. "Well, Terence, I'm caught in a bind. It is rather off for me to be asking this of you, but that first morning you and your father pitched in and helped the lady that runs this place." He paused to get the boy's reaction; so far, it seemed okay. "Well, she needs our help. For the life of me, I don't think I'll be any good at changing the linens on those beds, but I was wondering, do you have an idea how to get that job done?"

"You don't know how to make a bed?"

"Yes, I know how to make a bed, but there's probably more to cleaning a room than I'm accustomed to, this being a public place and all." He saw the slight grin as the boy ducked his head to hide it.

"Follow me, and I'll see if I can teach an old man new tricks." He didn't give Adam time to reply as he head down the hall to the first door and opened it to reveal a row of shelves stocked with bedding and towel goods. "Next stop the laundry room. I don't think Deidre's there yet. Let's hurry and get our supplies. We'll come back for the sheets and towels. I don't suppose you know how to iron?"

"Whoa, we may clean the room and make the bed but who says there has to be ironing done?"

Terence was shoving a mop, broom and a big bucket filled with cleaning items, into Adam's hands. "I bet your sheets are ironed, and you probably have monogramed pillowcases, don't you?" He handed Adam a pair of large rubber gloves and pulled a pair on, being careful the one covered the bandage on his hand. "Well, don't you?"

"Why would you think that?" Terence pulled the door shut behind them, led Adam to the first room. Knocked on the door, and when no one answered, opened the door to a room pretty much tumbled from one end to the other. He began to strip sheets off the bed, nodding with his head toward the bath area. Adam finally realized what the nod meant. He collected all the towels and wash cloths and threw them on top of the pile Terence had going by the door.

"Well, don't you?"

"What?" Adam was gawking at the words slashed across the mirror over the sink. Terence was quick to catch on. Shaking his head, he took one of the gray cloths from the bucket and wiped the mirror clean.

"You're too old to be reading those words." Terence went back to the bed, sprayed it with something that smelled like a disinfectant and asked again. "Don't you have monogrammed pillow-cases? You just as well tell me because I'll just ask again. I'd bet fifty dollars that you do."

"All right, young man, I do. So, what's that got to do with ironing?"

Terence held out a hand, palm up. "Put it there." Adam shook his hand, thinking it was a little late for that. "I mean a fifty. I won the bet."

"Ah, ha." Adam withdrew his hand. "I didn't bet."

"You said, All right." Terence burst into laughter. "I had you going there, didn't I?" He grinned. "Now we go collect the clean towels and sheets."

"Why don't we do strip downs first and then carry the clean items into the rooms? You think it needs disinfectant, so wouldn't that be appropriate?"

"How many times have you stayed in a motel and seen the maids do it that way?" Terence shook his head as though the task he had accepted, to work with Adam, was more than he bargained for. "What if Deidre suddenly had a new guest and needed a room that was ready, would she say, "oh, wait, we are in strip down mode, wait until I get the sheets on the bed, and then you can go in?"

"So, tell me, young sprout, where did you learn all this mumbo jumbo of how to do maid service?"

Terence laid a hand to his forehead feigning disgrace. "Oh, that's right, while you've been sleeping on your monogrammed and ironed pillowcases, I've been making a little spending money helping Deidre. And don't tell my dad, he'll bear down heavy on me when we get home."

"That's another thing, why haven't you and your dad left?"

"I wondered that myself, and then a little light went on inside of this masterpiece mind." Terence tapped his forehead. "Methinks, dear old dad is just a little smitten with that lady that patched up my hand." He had a way of shaking his head as if the world was a complicated place. "Don't get me wrong, she is nice, but he's not ready for that, besides, he doesn't excel as the world's best husband material."

I won't even go there, Adam was thinking, but he wasn't too pleased with the reason they were still there. He did look at the boy with more respect, to think he helped Deidre. That was a good thing. By the fifth room, he was becoming used to the nod of the head and the sarcasm when he failed simple test put before him by the teenage genius. Much to his chagrin, he did iron a few pillowcases.

"For the life of me, I can't understand why some of the pillow cases are as smooth as silk and others look like they're ravaged for life."

"There's a good reason," Terence replied. "Someone forgot to apply wrinkle control to the wash."

Adam blinked but they met new guest coming down the hall; after speaking they remained silent until they arrived at the next room.

"While I clean this one, if you will, go back to laundry with the dirty sheets and on the top shelf there's a purple can, Deidre called it lavender; it's purple and go to each room we cleaned, spray a bit, not too much and close the door and lock it and I'll be through here by the time you finish."

He did wonder that Terence didn't seem to want him in the last room and proceeded to find the purple can with the words lavender scent in small letters explaining why Deidre used it to freshen the rooms. Spraying a small amount as Terence instructed, he shut the door and returned to find the young man in the hall. "Do you want that I spray inside the last room you cleaned?" Terence shook his head, meaning, no.

"I think you will save Deidre embarrassment if you leave now," Terence, the boy genius was saying. "There's no need heaping more on her labyrinth of problems, is there?"

"What are Deidre's problems?" He asked.

"You don't know?" Terence seemed surprised. "I thought you and Deidre were great friends. She speaks of you with such respect."

"Well, that's nice to know, but I'm afraid I'm not…"

Terence interrupted, "I guess she didn't tell you she heard the motel had sold and she doesn't know if she will have a job."

Adam stood still, waiting for more, for some reason it seemed Terence was hiding his first thought but he reasoned, Deidre losing her job would be grounds for worry. "Who purchased the motel?"

"Someone in New York, I believe." Terence was aware that Adam was waiting for more. "Isn't that enough?"

"I suppose, but you make me feel there's more."

"If there is, time will tell, won't it?" A bit impatient, Terence pointed to the side door "See ya."

He stood there, staring at boy wonder, who was experienced it seemed in ignoring anyone over age twenty. When Terence started on down the hall, whistling, he gave up and left by the side door. Glancing at his wristwatch he realized it was time to either drive the lane to Nancy Ann's house to explain why they wouldn't be playing cards or some strange board game, due to Florence absence, or give in to the desire to forget the whole thing and slink off to his boy cave of a fifteen room house on the hill and enlarge on bad manners, his life had never allowed him to exercise.

Only minutes later he was knocking on the door. Jonathan invited him in. "Right on time." Turning he called toward the kitchen, "Hey, Nan, Adam's here." He pointed to the family room, "Go on in, the fire is just right, you know how sometimes you roast one side and freeze the other."

Nancy Ann joined them, a jug of apple cider, four glasses and a plate of molasses popcorn balls on a deep tray in her hands. "Hey, friend. I'm glad you made it. I can't reach Fleur. I thought she would come early but I haven't heard a word from her." He must have given away his anxiety in having to explain; both Nancy Ann and Jonathan gave him a questioning glance before they looked at each other. Nan spoke first, "She's not coming, is she? I knew she would try to get out of coming, but Fleur could never disappoint anyone, so I hoped that held true."

Adam was all nerves as Nancy Ann settled on the sofa by Jonathan, and said, "It's been years, Adam. I hope you can give her time to adjust to coming to grips with seeing you again."

"It's not that, Nan. I guess," he struggled with finding words to explain, "I don't even know where to begin with this crazy story." He realized sweat had broken out on his forehead and the palms of his hands felt damp.

"Listen, Adam, perhaps this is none of our business as I am making a guess it has to do with you driving Florence home last night." Nancy Ann had risen and was discreetly withdrawing to the kitchen, but Adam called to her.

"Don't leave, Nan. I need to try to explain what happened, to both of you. That's why I came. If you don't mind, I want to dig right in." Now, they listened. "Okay, it isn't easy." He took a deep breath. "She wasn't happy, in fact she gave me that cool treatment that you and I, Nan, know she does so well. She is an expert. And as we arrived at the Inn, she hopped out of the truck and walked in with me standing there pleading for her to listen. She ignored my calling her name. Needless to say, I did not sleep that night."

"Where is she? Did she leave?" Nancy Ann's eyes were wide with worry. "Usually she would tell me."

"The young man she patched up at the inn, the one who cut his hand to the bone, told me today she said she was reuniting with old memories. He assumed she meant people or at least a person."

"But she wasn't?" Nancy Ann was leaning forward.

"Let me fast forward, I was in same predicament. I arose early, ended up walking the mountain, all the way to the old rope bridge the three of us built, but I found it in shambles. Thinking it a danger to others I intended to cut it down, but I kept hearing the wind sound like someone in trouble and went to investigate. A foolish endeavor, I know, and dangerous for sure, crossing that foot path to the other side. What I found was a person in trouble, the boy with the cut hand had fallen in that chasm we always watched out for, and he knocked himself unconscious. I had a heck of a time pulling him to the top and then had to carry him that mile back to the house, after I did CPR. I found I'm not in as good a shape as I thought."

"A mile in frigid weather conditions would be hard on anyone, Adam. I couldn't do it," Jonathan replied.

"I called nine-one-one and they arrived shortly. They ignored anything I'd done, but they were professional."

"Evidently you both managed to help him, if he was speaking with you about Fleur, this morning."

"But, Nan, that's just it. It wasn't him and Fleur wasn't checking on an old acquaintance. It was Fleur, I rescued and carried, wearing the cap he had given her. I had no way of knowing. She was wearing those cover ups you sent over for your play day. I honestly thought I was carrying the boy."

"What?" Nancy Ann was on her feet, pacing before them. "So, is she badly hurt? Where is she?"

Jonathan heard the agony in Adam's voice as he replied, "I don't know. This morning, I drove over to the satellite location of Mercy Stinger. She was not registered. When the ambulance techs left my home, Fleur could have agreed to spend the night in my home. I promise you I would not have bothered her, but she wasn't there and that's why I believed she went with them."

"You don't know?" Nancy Ann's eyes had narrowed to a squinch. "Honestly, Adam, you are as gullible as ever." Jonathan, the man of the cloth, her husband, was giving her a please be careful look, but Nan was remembering private things only she knew about Florence.

"I went to sleep, sitting at the island, Nan, while the EMT's worked with her. I was that tired."

Something stirred in Nancy Ann's memory. She was weary from the talk, but what if she could find Fleur? What if her suspicions were right. Most of all, what if she'd had another medical emergency and no one was there to help her? Did she have meds with her?

"Adam. Stay here with Jonathan. I have a good idea where Fleur might be. Stay here." She was out of the room, grabbing a heavy coat from the closet, checking that there was a hat and gloves in the pocket. Taking keys from the tray by the door, she was gone before either man caught their breath. She ran to the old truck, fired it up and was backing out the drive, knowing they were gawking from the house window.

Snowplows had run. She made it down the lane, although the shadows were beginning to freeze the slush the plows left behind. She passed the road that led to the Inn, shaking her head at the young man's well-meaning story that Fleur was going to meet a person, when really, she was deluding his knowing she intended walking old paths with old memories. She made the turn that led to Adam's house. With the blink of an eye, she was there, where Fleur might be, now.

It dawned on her; back then, they had no idea what their future held. She had a brief recall of Adam removing the large decorative block by the back door, where a key was hidden and letting her and

Fleur in that day when he wanted to show Fleur his room upstairs. Good Lord, in heaven, she whispered, that was twenty years ago, no it was more. What was she thinking? And what had she done in those days while Adam wished to whisper sweet words in Florence ear? She had wandered outside. Later Fleur said they had only sat on the first steps of the stairway that led up to his room on third floor.

Oh, Florence, you were too quiet, too lady like and I can't see that you have changed. How in the world did we connect? I remember, Marge said, "opposites attract." Must be true…but if that was the case…neither Adam nor Florence put up much of a fight for each other. Now, she ran from the truck, up to the house, lift the block and began to breathe easier. The key, a bit rusted, was still there.

A lot of good she accomplished in the beginning with her own ex when his second wife died leaving a child she had not known about until he was two years old. She had barged right in to meet that child and created hostility…if ever a man's eyes had shot darts…she was laughing like a banshee as she entered the house and glanced up the stairs, climb those babies to third floor? Huh, uh. She would pass. But she didn't hesitate, closing the door, she made a dash through the rooms, but she didn't find Fleur. Returning to the one she thought Fleur would have chosen, she sit on the edge of the bed. The spread was a bit rumpled. Someone slept there. Leaning over she sniffed the pillow. She didn't recognize Fleur's perfume but there was a soft fragrance. She could go for that, Fleur would, too.

Making a quick glance for discarded clothing, and nothing visible, she walked through the house again. Something made her study the rooms more thoroughly. Slowly, she took in the colors, the furniture, the accent pieces and last she reasoned, most important, the painting over the fireplace mantle. A Peaceful Life, they had named it, discussing it to the bone, forgetting Florence had sit for the instructor and was there listening to every word. Now, she suspected

Adam purchased the painting when it went missing from the shop downtown, the shop Marge ran at the time but when she asked, Marge would not divulge the buyer. "I can't and you know that," she excused. "Don't ask again."

She had been in Adam's house the few times she was with Fleur but found she rather wander the yard, taking in all the plants his mother accumulated. She remembered thinking there was a lack of a green thumb and the plants and bushes were left to wander as she did. She could only wonder if Adam left any of those. Right now, they would be buried in snow.

There seemed always to have been a secretiveness about Adam's family. His father contributed to all the school program needs of the day, but Adam was not allowed in sports, even though the coach wanted him on the team. Another hushed item everyone questioned, away from his hearing, of course.

She was slowly coming to her senses. What was she doing in Adam's house and what was she thinking coming here alone, when Adam was standing right in front of her in her own home? Well, if Florence had been here, she wouldn't have wanted me to know, or talk to me in his presence. Now, why did she consider Florence being here? Wouldn't he have known? She hated going back to tell Jonathan and Adam she was wrong, Fleur wasn't where she thought… her actions were kind of impulsive.

She realized now, hindsight was a sharper tool than foresight! Well, in her defense, Adam said he slept through the whole thing, sitting on a stool at the island. That was a deep sleep. But if the med-techs suggested she go to the hospital, Fleur would resist and if they said she must be subdued for several hours, wouldn't that be just like Fleur to slip away quietly, shut the door to the world and go to bed, the usual pulling away from a disturbance, large or small. Fleur would not tell them where she went. Huh, uh, and come to think of it, neither would she. They could just wonder.

Now that she had everything figured out, she would just slink back to the truck, pray an essence of her father's wisdom lingered in the springs and coils of that ancient wonder to remind her to get this impulsive nature in control before someone brought her to task for it. Jonathan wouldn't. He was the wisest most considerate man she had ever known. Well, of the two she married, anyway, Jonathan was a prince.

So much for her friendzetic belief that she and Fleur still possessed such homing devices within their being they would know where the other was located if it was raining hail in a winter snowstorm and one couldn't see two feet in front of one's self. She should have known that talent was lost once a woman reached marrying age. Had Fleur ever married?

All she could do would be fold up her tent and go home. She prayed Adam would have left and she could curl up beside Jonathan and soak up his abundant goodness and mercy. She was tired. No, she was exhausted.

* * * * *

Chapter 8

Florence heard a vehicle pull into the drive and panicked. She had climbed the flight of stairs, curious to see if Adam's room was as described when they were teenagers. Why had his parents thought a three-story house appropriate for a rural country setting such as Mosby?

"They were from France," Adam had explained. "Mother's family home was handed down generation to generation and Father loving her as he did, wanted her to reside in opulence reminisce of the home land." There, he always shook his head. "If it were me, I would have studied the landscape that stretches throughout Mosby and built a two-story Currier and Ives.'

"Look at us," she had whispered, "in our teens. What do we know of building houses?"

"Should I inherit my parent's home and ever a new roof needs installing," Adam declared, taking pencil and paper and sketching a house, "I will alter the third floor by raising the roof, placing dormers here and here and Mosby will have a Currier and Ives home in its neighborhood." They had laughed as they sit on a stone bench in the orchard, staring at his home. Now, as she stood silently waiting and listening for a door to open, she realized he had done exactly as he said. The roof was a high pitch with dormers, but inside the attic space was a finished room she supposed once belonged to Adam, no longer used but there if needed. It was a beautiful home. Evidently, a beautiful house did not make a happy home.

Silent, not bending a knee, she stood listening wondering if it was Adam and what he had forgotten or perhaps it was lunch time. If not Adam, would it be a housekeeper that would stay a length of time. She heard doors open and close and finally someone leaving. She dared not go to the window that had no cover of curtain, lest she would be seen. When she felt certain the vehicle had cleared the yard and headed down the lane, she started down the stairs.

Where had she left the cover-ups from the day before? She remembered the medical people pulling them from her body. She found them stuffed in the washer in the laundry room. What would she wear? Not the long gown. She would retrieve her underwear from yesterday she had stuck under her pillow before sleeping. She studied the closet adjacent the washer and dryer and opening the door saw a stack of washed denims and flannel shirts. She could make do. But would she find her cell phone intact after all she had been through or was it lying at the bottom of the chasm? Going through the dirty clothes in the washer she found a card the grumpy man had given her the day before but no cell. Studying his name, she returned to the kitchen and found a house phone and dialed his number.

"Ray Bollinger." She recognized his voice as she stood there wondering about her medicine.

"Hi, Ray. Florence Stokely here. I wonder if you are out and about and could do me a little favor?" She listened. "Ray, we didn't have a formal introduction. I bandaged your son's hand yesterday." She gave a faint chuckle. "Yes, Florence, as in Nightingale. Yes."

"Truth is, I wandered a bit far from the Inn and I wonder if you would pick me up. Yes, where the road makes a Y and goes up to the big house on the hill. I'll wait by the rock with the family crest. Sure thing. Thanks."

Folding the night clothes, she placed them in one of the empty bureau drawers and then dressed in the borrowed clothing, found the boots she'd worn the day before and Terence's red cap and retrieved an insulated jacket she'd seen in the closet. She was ready to hike down to the end of the lane. Unnoticed, she had slept in Adam's home and unnoticed she was leaving.

Within minutes she was sliding onto the seat of Ray's Land Rover. "I'm very appreciative you would come pick me up." Glancing at the dash of the Rover, she saw it was three o'clock.

"No problem," Ray replied. "I was returning from Cookeville when you called. This is but a skip and a hop out of the way, but where are your wheels?"

Florence gave a self-conscious laugh, "you must not know, I'm on the MIA list. I roamed too far from the Inn and actually spent the night with a friend, whose automobile is snowed in but I wasn't sure I could walk all the way back to the Inn and I did have your card, so I called you."

"I imagine the girl at the Inn is missing you, then. I left early this morning," he added.

"Deidre?" Florence sighed. "She seems like a hard worker, and there's plenty of work."

"Yeah. Some of the guests were grumbling service was poor."

Florence appeared thoughtful. "She did tell them she would refund their money if they wanted to drive on across the mountains."

"They would have been back. I understand the roads were closed last night. Still, the Inn needs some serious work done on it. I don't get the owner leaving during busy season." He sighed, settling into the seat. "They should just push it in and start all over again."

"Why would you say that?"

"Just one man's opinion," he said, shrugging his shoulders. "Just an opinion."

She breathed a sigh of relief once they were in the Inn's parking lot. "Thanks," she said, extending a hand. He smiled and stooped to kiss her hand instead of shaking it.

"It was the least I could do. You did take care of my boy."

Florence was relieved to not encounter Deidre on the way to her room. Something unsatisfying had entered her mind, when Ray Bollinger remarked the Inn should be pushed in.

* * * * *

Searching through the suitcase she found the little black book that contained business information and made the call. The gentleman at the other end of the line seemed hesitant to discuss the property she had committed to purchase and this bothered her further. What information did Ray Bollinger hold that had been hidden in the original contract. Could he be the other person vying for the property she and Matthew had discussed?

She was out of her league. By the time she googled the entities presented by the Investment company, she was weary and only heard the chime of the lobby clock through a fog of unanswered questions and suspicions that she had bit off more than she could chew, so to speak, in purchasing the plot of land she thought would bring comfort as she made what she thought her last life change. It was her intent to enjoy the days of retirement as she looked into the future, with a degree of income she could build on and being a person of great energy, she had known there must be something with a degree of daily attention to keep her from falling into depression from lack of being occupied. Such had been her life, she could not at this age give in to sitting day after day in a rocking chair, knitting.

The last thought gave her a needed chuckle as if to say, yes, you will be accountable to yourself, and thank God your sense of humor is returning. The ordeal of falling in the chasm and knocked unconscious had obviously taken its toll on her. And, then, there was Adam. What to do about Adam. He didn't deserve forgiveness. He was the one ended their relationship. Why had she felt the martyr? He was the one destroyed their plans to marry. Who did he think he was wanting her to forget past hurts and consider him again? No, he did not deserve a second chance and neither did she deserve to be thought of with pity. She couldn't stand being pitied.

With renewed energy she glanced at the bedside clock. Nancy Ann ask they have dinner around five and she had no other place to go. She could make it. It was not her character to get even, so to speak, but Adam's punishment now seemed prominent in her mind. She would attend the dinner with her friends and in the process perhaps make Adam aware of what he lost when he did not stand up for his own happiness those long years past, marrying another woman just to give a child that was not his own a name. More than twenty years had passed, but now, Florence completely dismissed the persuasion of his parents and lay the blame at Adam's feet.

* * * * *

It was ten minutes to five when she knocked on the door and Nancy Ann pulled her inside.

"Where have you been? I've been going crazy over you. They said you were hurt and possibly in the hospital. I've called every hospital within two hundred miles."

"Hello, to you, too." Florence pulled herself free as they pushed through the door. "And, you have been busy, if you called all the hospitals within two hundred miles."

Nancy Ann spewed air between her lips, looking somewhat as crazy as she felt at the moment. So great was her relief. "I was afraid you wouldn't come. I have been going crazy."

"Hmm," Florence managed, pushing back as Nancy Ann hugged her tightly to her chest. "You are a piece of work, my friend.

Truly. I would have thought you would know exactly how I was feeling and where I was." She was elated to see Nancy Ann's embarrassment was as heavy as a child's. So, it was Nancy Ann had come to Adam's house.

"Well, I thought you would be at Adam's, that maybe he wasn't aware you were there. He's been in such a daze himself." She was pulling Florece toward the kitchen. "I actually thought we would still have those vibes and I went to his house, broke in, I guess you'd say, and I did think once you might have been in the bedroom…but he had come earlier and said you were taken in the ambulance, as far as he knew, by the medical people from Mercy."

"Breathe." Florence illustrated taking deep breaths. "You have worked yourself into a tizzy."

"Tizzy?" Nancy Ann realized the stove's timer was in rhythm with her thumping heart. "Yes, I guess, a tizzy," she said as she pushed a button and the noise stopped. "Here, let me take your coat. Sit down there and fill me in. The men are out back looking at Jonathan's fifty-seven Chevrolet." Suddenly, she laughed. "I am so happy to see you. Now, where were you?"

The back door opening, followed by robust voices and removal of heavy outer wear saved Florence. Eyebrows raised, she met Nancy Ann's stare, that said, now how are you going to handle this? Faking a laugh, she said, "breathe, remember, you have to breathe to exist."

"Is that what I'm doing? Existing? And what about you my soul mate, what about you?"

There was an awkward moment, as the men entered the room and she and Adam made eye contact, but Florence quickly cast attention on Jonathan. "So, you have a fifty-seven Chevrolet? Why is that important to you?"

Jonathan grinned. "It was my dad's old car. Somehow, he salvaged it through the years and when I saw how much it meant to him, I helped restore it and when he died…" Jonathan paused, "it wasn't that I'd tied up a lot of money in the restoration, but that he and I made so many good memories during that time…I just couldn't let it go." His smile deepened, "and our girl, here," he hugged Nancy Ann. "Had this shed with her dad's old truck in it and she said there's room for one more." He kissed Nan's forehead. "It all just happened to come together."

"Ah, yes, the memories. That's why you saved it and now you revisit it." Florence nodded.

"Yeah, I do. My father was a wonderful man and taught me a lot of good life standards." He hugged Nancy Ann, "and I find memories sometimes ease the soul. What do you think?"

"Excuse me," Nancy Ann interrupted. "Adam and I are here, too, listening to you two, but the food is ready, if we could enjoy it while it's hot and those yeast rolls are to die for, if I must say so, myself."

"The rolls are excellent," Adam said a short time, later. "You are a wonderful cook."

"Do you cook, Adam?" Jonathan asked, rising to collect plates, ready to help Nancy Ann bring in the black berry cobbler. He paused, waiting for Adam's reply.

"As a matter of fact, I do."

Surprised, Florence heard the words pop out of her mouth. "You…cook? Why?"

"Honest? You want the honest reply?" His eyes met hers in challenge. "I cook because the woman I married did not."

"What did she do, wait for the maid? I assume you had a maid, a butler, who knows what else."

"She did very little, except in the beginning she did take care of her little daughter, but then she tired of that responsibility and I found myself filling in there, too." His serious expression bore down on Florence. "Is that what you want? To know how it was for me all those years, when I married her to save my parents? And you won't forgive me?"

Suddenly, she realized they were discussing private thoughts, no doubt held between them, never expressed due to their promise to each other to never seek search or try to find one another. "I'm sorry," she managed to utter. "These things are best left alone. I apologize."

Adam's face held a strange resolve. "You would not let me tell you in private. Here, before friends, I will tell you I have paid dearly for the decision I made to marry Charlotte. I was young, and told my parents would suffer serious persecution in their world of business and the people with which they associated. Do you think I haven't wished a million times I'd done differently?"

"It's in the past," she managed to reply. "Why have this discussion now?"

"Because I've never stopped loving you. I want your forgiveness and an opportunity to build a friendship of sorts, if you insist, we start at the bottom." He leaned across his plate, staring into her face. "Florence, we have another lifetime to live, even at this age. Give me a chance."

Suddenly, she remembered all the years of longing for this man, the hurt of being passed over for a girl he had barely known. Rejection had killed her spirit for a time, but raising his son, alone, she found the determination she needed to excel. Now, that hurt reappeared, tenfold.

She was aware, Nancy Ann and Jonathan had withdrawn discreetly to the back room, allowing them the privacy they deserved. She arose, taking her plate across the room, returning to look Adam in the eye. "It doesn't matter, now, Adam. The past is what it is. You don't owe me an apology or explanation."

He appeared crestfallen. "We won't be together, unless you allow it, Fleur." He said her name softly, as she remembered. She was silent. Hadn't she longed, then, to hear his voice?

"I've been working on refurnishing the family home, according to the plans you and I made those many years ago." He sighed, wearily. "It seemed right, I felt a strange release removing all the old furniture, those obtuse paintings Mother allowed the designer to hang. There's something I'd like to show you one day, if you will allow me. I'm not ashamed to say I have hope you will lose this anger toward me, and see, for yourself, what we planned was good….as we were." His eyes were pleading. "Give us a chance."

She heard the clink of dishes from the adjoining room. No doubt Nancy Ann was collecting dishes for dessert. "Adam, lets save ourselves this discussion and try our best to compliment friends that have invited us into their home, who have only our best interests at hand."

"Agreed," he said, rising, but she took the plate from his hand and carried it to the sink as Nancy Ann and Jonathan returned carrying the black berry cobbler and dessert dishes.

"Anyone ready for dessert?" The silence was heavy. "I tell you what," Jonathan said. "Let's clear the table, spend a few minutes trying to breach this moment and later, if we want it, the dessert will be right here."

* * * * *

The evening was ruined, as far as Florence was concerned. Finally, unable to stand it any longer, she stood. "Thank you all for a lovely dinner. I believe I'll head home and to bed."

Nancy Ann walked with her to the door. Hugging Florence, she whispered, "I'm sorry. Call me if you need me or want to talk."

Adam was loath to stay. He blew out a heavy breath. "I'm really sorry you had to hear my undying love to Florence, but she wasn't going to listen to me, otherwise." He rose up to pace a bit in front of the fireplace. "All I said was true. You may not know this, but as Florence was ready to leave for college and our plans to marry were intact, my parent's friends came to visit, needing a husband for their daughter who was pregnant. I was the chosen one to replace the scoundrel who left her high and dry because they wanted to save her reputation."

Pacing again, he said, "it was never a marriage but I was caught in a role I neither wanted or was good at and she kept in touch with the father of her child. It was never meant to be." He sighed. "When Florence came here, the last time, I realized as I had always thought, that I never stopped loving her. My wife, so to speak, never measured up to Fleur. We divorced before we came to hate each other." Bittersweet, sadness and anger entwined to flood all he was as a man. "I better leave," he said. "They say grown men shouldn't cry."

* * * * *

Florence drove the lane, remembering Adam's words. "I never stopped loving you, Fleur. I want your forgiveness and if we must start all over and build with friendship, I want that, too."

If he loved her so much, why had he waited twenty years to tell her? She wondered how many years he had been alone. He mentioned the child. She understood the child was a little girl. She could imagine that child wrapping Adam around her finger. She saw him reading a book, playing tea parties and all kind of things most men wouldn't do, but he would. Why, then was she so angry towards him? She had been when first she had Matthew and was alone to take care of all his needs, but this anger? She questioned herself. She always thought she was a fair person, but this? She was at a loss. Was it her age? The fact she thought she was returning to a place she visited as a teenager and fell in love with the rural setting and the ways of the people? Or, in her heart, did she remember loving Adam? If that were the case, why this anger that he was so late in life telling her of his unrequited love.

* * * * *

The bed table phone rang early the next morning. "Are you awake?"

"Nancy Ann? Why are you calling this early?"

"I wanted to know how you are, last night must have been rough on you. Besides, I thought you rose early to help prepare breakfast."

"Oh." Florence slid out of bed, grabbing a pair of denims, hurrying into the bathroom to comb her hair and press it into a bun on top of her head. "I was so tired; I must have slept like the dead and I did forget I help with breakfast. Let me go, Deidre will wonder what happened to me."

"What did you decide about Adam?"

"Nothing. Absolutely nothing, except not to be caught dead in his presence. He is twenty some years too late."

"It takes a bold man to express his love in front of others. Jonathan said he was a brave man."

"I've got to go, Nan. Entertain yourself on my behalf. Love you. Bye." Florene hung up the phone and hurried down the hall to find Deidre' placing a pan of biscuits in the oven. "Morning," she said, taking condiments from the shelf to sit on each table. "How are you?"

Deidre nodded and turned her face away from Florence view, but Florence saw the girl had been crying. Guest were beginning to enter the room; Ray Bollinger, among them, followed by Terence, wearing a baseball cap. Florence decided she would not ask questions.

"Morning, Beautiful," Ray said. "I believe it's Florence, as in Nightingale. Right?" Terence rolled his eyes. "Need any help?" She motioned to the coffee station. With a definite smirk that belied he could do that, Ray claimed the station, making small talk with the guests. She wondered if he actually enjoyed the interaction. It seemed the guest enjoyed his endless tirade.

Terence took a seat near the television, listening to the latest weather report. "You okay, Terence?" She leaned down to see his eyes beneath the baseball cap. "Hey, what's that? You have a black eye?"

"Yes, I do, but you don't have to announce it." He defended his right to privacy.

Hands up, Florence said, "I'm sorry I hit a sore spot. What can I get you? To make up for my mistake?" She laid a hand on his shoulder. "Come on, Bud, you know I like you." His rigid composure did not lessen. "Wanna tell me how it happened?"

"No."

"Ouch." She moved on, curious, but determined to avoid him throughout the breakfast hour.

Somehow, working together, they made it. Afterwards, Terence slunk out to avoid contact or help with the dishes. Ray seemed bent on raising opinion of himself joking with Deidre as he took place at the wash station, but Florence noticed Deidre' was lost in her own world and by her countenance Florence decided it wasn't good. She ended up drying the plates and rinsing the stemware in vinegar water to give them a shine, while Deidre' cleaned the coffee station.

"Guess you noticed," Ray whispered, "our hostess is down in spirit." Florence shrugged. "Come on," Ray said in a low voice. "She's depressed and I don't blame her, I would be too, if I was her."

"The ships not sinking," Florence reminded him. "We all tried to help. We did our part."

"There's more to it than that?"

"Like what? Supply not arriving, or what?"

"Worse. Supplies are arriving but Deidre' had an event planned that has fallen through and now she's stuck with all the supplies to have a five-star party and she doesn't have enough storage to save them." He paused, "Nor money to pay for them."

Florence stepped back to see Ray better. "What do you mean? And how do you know this?"

"I have my sources. I'm not here just by chance. True, I was on the way to take Terence to a game, but the conditions of the roads led us to this place and amazingly enough it has been on my radar awhile."

Florence studied him. "You are an enigma of surprises. I don't quite know how to take you." She waited for him to elaborate, but he just smiled, mysteriously. "Do you care to explain?"

Ray evaded her question with oner of his own. "At the moment, what do you think? Should we try to help her out?"

"Wait. I need more than this. I don't understand how you know the inside workings of Deidre."

His hands went up, in defense. "Terence is the one with the inside information, not me."

"What about Terence? How did Terence get the black eye? He's avoiding me."

Ray became quiet, seeming busy with the cleaning of the morning kitchen. Florence let it rest, if the occasion presented its self she would speak with Deidre.'

She was on her way out when she and Deidre, coming from opposite directions, rounded the doorway to the hall and bumped into each other. Deidre let out a little yelp and began to sob. Florence, opened her arms and Deidre fell into them.

"Oh, my dear, come aside, let's see what's going on and if we can do anything to correct it."

Evidently, Deidre' was at her wits end. "Oh, Miss Florence," she said. "I had this event planned to help bring income in to the Inn. Galant gives me full reign when he leaves to Florida each winter and I do the best I can but this time I booked an event and now the weather has brought a close to that and I have all these supplies arriving. I don't know what to do."

Florence listened. "Deidre', let me think on this. Go ahead and prepare for the dinner hour and I'll see if there's a way." For a minute she wondered her own audacity to consider how to help this girl out of her misery. Deidre left her with hope and she went to her room to ponder her own advice to this girl.

Little did Florence know, Adam had arrived. He had purposely avoided the breakfast hour but something pulled him in to check out the situation. He had not rest, as usual, and had risen early trying to do odd jobs, long left undone, in order to keep his mind at bay. Florence wanted nothing to do with him. What was he to do, return to New York, a life of a lone bachelor with no one at all to care whether he lived or died? So, went his own pity party until he gave up and drove to the Inn.

One glance Deidre's way and he saw the parlor of the girl; Pale and seeming sad. He approached her. "How's it going?"

Deidre, thinking Mr. Adam and Miss Florence were old friends that had probably been in communication and discussed her problem, replied, "It's not good, Mr. Adam, but Miss Florence has agreed to think on my dilemma and possibly come up with a way to help me fix it. If you could lend her a hand, I would be ever so grateful." She pointed to the kitchen, "I'm finishing up here. She told me to keep my mind on the dinner hour and she would work on it." Diedre' sighed. "I'm at my wits end, Mr. Adam, but if you think of how the woman has helped me during this snow storm, coming in here unannounced off the highway, it's like God sent an angel. I want to thank you, too, for the morning you took care of the guest with credit cards. That was a big help. My people not able to come in to work, just about got me."

"Do you have Miss Florence room number that I might contact her?"

* * * * *

Chapter 9

Florence made the bed. She had not seen any of Deidre's workers in the hall that led to the laundry. What would it take to have a full crew during snow storms if the Inn was up and running properly? She could not dismiss Ray's comment from the days before, it was his opinion the Inn should be pushed in. She had not told Matthew that bit of news. By now her bid was in, surely accepted and the paper work underway. Glancing down at her hastily donned clothes in order to be in the great room helping Deidre' with breakfast, she decided she should change. Surely, the snow plows would have cleared a path through the community.

If there was no further snow, she would go into the business section, and possibly find Marge's shop. Noticing her clothing had the smell of eggs and bacon, she decided a shower was in order. A few minutes later, toweled and feeling fresh, she found a gray pair of slacks, a filmy silver pullover and was just finishing her make up when the phone rang. Hurrying to spray a mist of cologne behind her neck and the pullover's front V, she stared at it a moment, thinking only Deidre' would call the room. Busy in front of the mirror, putting silver hoops in her ears, she answered.

"Hi, Deidre' are you feeling better?"

There was a pause and then a male voice said, "Fleur?" She felt a trickle of surprise.

"Adam?"

"Yes, Deidre' gave me the number and Fleur…" He paused, letting her adjust to the idea it was him. "Fleur…." He was having difficulty, unable to see her expression, he said quickly, "Don't hang up, I understand from Deidre' there's a problem of sorts. She didn't tell me what, exactly, but she had some notion that you and I talk and possibly I could help with the problem."

"That won't be necessary, Adam." Florene replied in a clipped voice. "I've not had time to think it through, myself, but I'm sure we will come up with something. Rest assured, we will."

"Fleur?" He called her name but had no inkling of what might persuade her to join him.

"You haven't changed, Adam. You always ask a question with a long space in between your words. What else?" He was silent. "Adam, you called. Remember. What do you want?"

"I want to help Deidre'. I can tell something is bothering her. Could we meet and talk?"

Florence was drumming her fingernails on the bedside table as she sank down on the bed. "I have no idea how you and I could come to agreement on anything…."

"Please, Fleur, not for me or for you, but for a very deserving, hard-working young woman."

"What do you have in mind?" She took a deep breath. "But, it's not a good idea to discuss this here." For some reason, although Ray knew there was a problem, she didn't want him part of the discussion, and he had a way of being around at the most ill-timed moments.

"Nothing opens until noon when we have snow," Adam explained. "Would you consider I pick you up and we go to my house?" She was quiet. It seemed forever. Finally, he said, "Fleur, would you consider going to my house? I'll pick you up and bring you back." He was struggling for a reason she might. "Wouldn't it be nice to tour the shops together and see how things have changed?"

He could feel her refusal. "I promise not to bring up matters that concern us, only helping Deidre'." He glanced at the clock on the desk. She was silent. "I'm in the lobby."

Florence sighed, as though it was a burden and he caught the sound.

"All right, I'll be right down. But you have to remember your promise."

"Scouts honor," he replied. "I'll bring the truck up to the door."

Stepping into black ankle boots, she chose a long heavy sweater coat, found her purse and was out the door. Hadn't she sworn she would not be caught dead in Adam Chatham's presence? Then, what was she doing now? "God only knows," she whispered.

* * * * *

She found him standing ready to open the door and see her inside the truck.

"How about we drive through the shop section while they are closed and come back this afternoon, maybe even find your friend. What was her name?"

"Marge? She was more Nan's friend; I was just included summers I visited."

"I bought a large painting from her. It hangs over the fireplace."

"Perhaps I will see it, then." She hoped he never realized she had seen it.

"Yes." He replied. "I treasure the painting and it replaced one only God knows what the meaning of that one was, Mother was extremely happy to see the replacement."

"Oh, she saw it?"

"Yes, before she died." He smiled. "I guess that was obvious, wasn't it?"

Nan's resolution to be firm and stern, slipped. She smiled. "Yes, I guess it was."

"Thanks, Fleur. I want us to relax and let go the animosity that seemed to rear up between us. It's nice to see you smile."

She ignored the compliment. "You and Charlotte had no children?"

He gave her a curious glance. "Charlotte and I never consummated our marriage, Fluer."

She was shocked. "All those years?"

"Charlotte stayed in touch with her child's father. That was grounds enough to know she never cared for me and in order to keep the money flowing from her parents she honored the marriage by staying in it to keep them safe from the threat, the reason we married."

"I wondered if you fathered many children, or I should say any child, I suppose."

"No, sadly, I did not. I suppose like any man I would treasure a son to carry our name, but I found Charlotte's little girl a sweet delight and I was a good father to her, even though she was not mine, but Charlotte left and took her and I am sure I will never see her again."

"That's sad. I'm sure she remembers you. My Aunt was always so kind to invite me during summer and Nancy Ann was good to accept me. I hope I didn't infringe on her friendship."

"I would never have met you, Fleur, had you not come to Mosby those years."

She gave him a condescending glance.

He laughed. "Was that out of line?" Now he grinned, "Just pretend I didn't say it. What do you think of the improvements to the artsy section of Mosby?" They slid past the moment of his remark and rode through Main Street, taking the first turn that led back to the highway and eventually to Adam's home. She was out of the truck and by his side before he round the vehicle.

"You don't have to be such a gentleman, Adam."

"I don't? Well, I always remember you as a lady, Fleur, and I would like to make a good impression." She shook her head, raising a finger to tap the air. "Did I say too much?" He made a monkey face. In spite of her resolve, she laughed as he opened the door and said, "Come on in."

Taking the sweater coat he said, "you look great, Fleur. Come let me show you something in the gathering room." She followed knowing, but again resolute not to give away she had seen his home. He led her into the room with the fireplace and the painting she had sit as model, those many years past. "I bought it from Marge," he said. "After Charlotte left, I knew I couldn't stand the house the way it was. She never cared because her interest was elsewhere. We suffered all those years until her parents died. A terrible thing to say, but she had her reason for staying and I made do, loving Amy." For a moment it seemed sadness claimed him.

"Amy was the little girl?" She stared at the painting. "You know I sit for that painting?"

"That's why I bought it. I was always afraid someone else would take a fancy to it."

"You were loyal to Charlotte?" He nodded. "I'm at a loss to understand your choice of...."

He interrupted, "I think you know why I wanted this painting. Let me say, this, when Charlotte left, I started clearing the house of memories of our years together and brought in new items." He sighed deeply. "I don't know if it helped or not, but it gave me hope."

Florence turned toward the large island in the next room where last she had seen Adam, his head on folded arms, sleeping soundly. That night she had bathed, toured his home, examined the clothing in the bureau drawers in the room where she slept and he had never known she was there.

"Why don't we discuss why we are here, Adam? I'm not fully aware of the problem with Deidre, but Ray, remember the father of the boy whose hand I bandaged? He said Deidre had planned an event, but the weather has prevented it's happening as the roads are still too dangerous to travel. In fact, many are still blocked, over the mountain. Long story short, she has all the supplies arriving, no place to store them and a great financial loss."

"So that's it?" He huffed a great breath and took the seat opposite her. "How does this man, Ray, have an inner ear to Deidre's problems? She and I have been friends a while and she never mentioned any of this, to me."

"Terence, Ray's son, has the inner ear, not Ray."

"There's something about him," Adam shook his head. "I shouldn't say that? I don't even know the man…but he is abrasive at times and rubs people the wrong way."

"Yes, I saw that, but he did pitch in and help, though he would not go up the hill to the club for water that night."

"I wondered about that. So, what is your plan?" He pulled a spiral book from the center of the island and took a pen from his shirt pocket. "Why don't we list a few positive and negative aspects to the Inn and what we possibly could do to help her out."

"One thing bothers me; Ray mentioned the Inn has need of many repairs and his opinion is it should be pushed in." She noticed he was sketching even as they talked.

"Demolished?" This seemed to surprise Adam. "I know it needs a few improvements but it is actually the last stop before heading across the mountains. A lot of folks don't want to drive the route after dark and stop in Mosby. That is also beneficial to the many art and hobby shops. In fact, that is how many of the owners make their living. Through time they've improved what they stock, for that very reason."

"The Inn is not large enough to accommodate as many as stopped in during this snow storm."

"No, but there are several bed and breakfast. The problem there, is the owners are getting older and have mentioned closing within the next five years, which would make the Inn a more profitable business. It's Galant, that strays to the sunshine state every winter and leaves Deidre' on her own. That is why she has the event, whatever profit is made, he gives to her, his way of thanking her for running the business while he is away."

"As I understand he is ready to retire, but she cannot purchase the Inn, but still needs employment?" When he nodded, she continued. "Then, it is your opinion, the Inn has a future? The location is good and being the last overnight stay before crossing the mountains, you see a profitable investment?"

"Where else would they go? They reach this point, knowing the Inn has been here as they come south each year…come travel this route each year, but if it's gone they have to go on over the mountain."

"That being the case, who did Deidre' cater to? Surely, those she invited were beneficial to the Inn and vice versa."

"In your travels, haven't you seen the roadside advertisement of what lies ahead? That's how Deidre' came up with the idea. The obscure places of business look to her to place their brochures here in the Inn. That way, many travelers take side road trips and it benefits all. Her annual event brings everyone together to discuss what is needed, but heavy rains and then the snowstorm are not our usual weather and it slowed business this year. Snow, yes, but not the rain. In planning the event, the date became later and later. Usually she tries for Labor Day."

"So, you did know there was a problem?"

"Maybe, but Deidre' is not one to complain and she kept hoping the problem would lighten. What I didn't know was that she had ordered all the supplies. That means food that will spoil, and at a hefty price."

"What can we do?" A glimmer of understanding was taking hold. "Did she plan the event around any theme?"

"You mean like Easter or Christmas?" Adam stared at her, thinking, "No, but we could."

"Do the citizens of Mosby still raise gardens? I remember pumpkins and gourds this time of year, well, they weren't ready for harvest when I left for home, but I saw a lot of produce in those days." She studied his sketch, "Weren't there apple orchards and what else?"

"There are pumpkin patches." He wasn't sure he was understanding, completely. "You mean decide a theme, for this time of year, maybe harvest?"

"Yes, and go with it, let the people of Mosby sell themselves in order to save Deidre and possibly the Inn, in some strange way." She reached for the spiral notebook. "Who would the people of Mosby be able to invite? It would have to be points of interest where the roads are open." She held the notebook out and studied the sketch. "Is that the Inn? Improved?"

A bit sheepish, he nodded, "yeah, someone tried to talk me into taking it on, once when Galant swore, he was going to put it on the market and move to Florida, but anyone that has watched Deidre' work, knows she deserves consideration, and he put the idea on hold. I, did consider it overnight, even drew out plans to enlarge the capacity, but when he withdrew his idea, I also withdrew mine. However, it may be out for sale, and we don't even know."

She avoided him by not looking up. "So, we build on a harvest theme, place banners along the highway, say fifty miles out, contact radio and make sure it is on local Face Book, and we set a date for a townhall meeting to inform the citizens of Mosby, what we are trying to do."

"What exactly are we planning?" He grinned. "I know in general, but our main goal is…."

"To set Mosby back on the map, to be an important stopping off place before going over the mountains and in so doing, we will have a big celebration, sell tickets for the dinner Deidre' will prepare, hire a guest speaker and all in all have a grand opening for the future of Mosby Inn."

They were in the truck headed back to the Inn when she glanced at the notebook sketch. turning to Adam she said, "You always liked sketching buildings. Didn't you plan to take classes in architecture, in college?"

"I actually did," he admitted. "My parents were set on me excelling in business education to help our holdings in New York, but as a secondary I did study what was dear to my heart."

"Have you done anything with it?"

He smiled, "have you heard of the Echo building in New York? The Downtree branch office in New Jersey?" She nodded. "Those are mine. I never told the folks. I figured why worry them?"

"Aren't you the one? Things you have kept to yourself, but seem to bring great satisfaction."

"Fleur, don't we all have something we hold dear to ourselves that no one else knows about?" He wanted to reach across and squeeze her hand, instead he gripped the steering wheel.

"Yes," she whispered. "I suppose we do." She thought of Matthew and for a moment remorse claimed her, that she and Adam had never completed the plans they made in their youth, knowing now, they never would.

His next words went straight too her heart. "I am sorry our plans were ruined by my parents. I imagine you have blamed me all these years, but Fleur, what would you have done if your parent's lives were at stake? Would you have saved them, in spite of your own happiness?"

"I don't know, Adam. I wasn't the one, you were. I only know as a young woman I was devastated."

"But we had that night together, Fleur. I never forgot. I hoped you still cared. Was I foolish to have carried that with me all these years?" Almost a whisper, he finished, No one ever spoke comfort to me, ever as you did that night. Somehow, I knew I could go on, because you said I would. Sometimes I wondered what it would have been like, a family with you, Fleur? We could have had a son." Almost beyond himself, he turned to her. "Why is it too late for us?"

A nervous sound escaped her lips, "Adam, you promised. Don't ruin the evening. We made plans to try to save Deidre and the Inn, let's you and I do our best to see this through."

He sobered, straightening his shoulders as though the motion would improve his state of mind. "I'll do my best, Fleur." He would take the only opportunity offered to be with her. "One thing, if you will, explain why is that Ray fellow staying around? I understood from Terence, they were headed for a game, but the weather ruled that out, why are they not headed home?"

"You said the roads ahead are closed beyond the Mercy Stiger exit, are they open the other direction?" He nodded, turning into the Inn's drive. "I don't know. They wouldn't be affected returning to their home, would they?" She sighed, "He is different. It's Terence won my heart. He's a brave boy, but he misses his mother."

"Terrence has ingenuity." Adam chuckled. "Did you know he is Deidre's main co-worker?"

"What do you mean?"

"He is the force behind the clean rooms required for new guests stopping in." Laughter welled up from the bottom of his ribs. "Right down to a slight squirt of lavender, his words."

"And you know this, because?"

"I helped him when the Inn was desperate. I still don't know how I got rooked in." For the first time, Florence laughed, the warm melodic sound he remembered. He slid from the seat and was around to her side, opening the door for her as she leaned down to pick up the notebook she had dropped. Turning, and a bit unsettled, her foot slipped on the automatic foot board and she tumbled off into Adam's arms. In the moment required to regain equilibrium, she found herself looking into his eyes, a smile of satisfaction on his lips and the humor they had just shared giving him a rested look that had always touched her heart. For a moment, she thought he was going to kiss her and in a wild unplumbed way she wished he would, but as quickly as the inkling had crossed her mind, she pulled away from his body.

"Sorry," she said, "My mother didn't name me Grace. I lost my footing."

"Don't apologize, I enjoyed it," he replied, a rakish gleam in his eyes. "Let's do it again."

"Adam. You would never have said that as a boy. You were the epitome of nice manners."

His laughter rose, victoriously. "Imagine, Fleur, that small incident made me happy. What do you suppose would happen if you let down your guard and let me hold your hand or heaven only knows, should I kiss you. I thought about it, you know, but I didn't want you to slap me."

"You are crazy. You would never have taken advantage of me as a boy." Her eyes snapped, dangerously piercing as she stared at him. "Why are you doing this?"

"I'm a man, Fleur," he sobered, quickly. "I will do everything I can to win you over. If you want me to be a stiff, stilted gentleman, I will, but I much prefer we accept there's a reason we are here. Why can't you quit trying to punish me for things that happened twenty years ago."

"Are you finished?" She started up the drive toward the sidewalk that was beginning to freeze again in the late evening temperature. "If we are to work together, you will have to quit this nonsense, or I'll ask Terence and his father to help me."

"Really?" A flash of anger crossed his face. "You would hurt me like that? Did I mortally wound you, Fleur? Are you so hard and bitter you won't forgive? Do you prefer to live the rest of your life unrelenting, when God has brought us to the same little town at the same time…"

She turned, a mix of disbelief and perturbed dislike of his words on her face. The action was too much on the iced walk, she was flailing as he caught her and brought her up fast and hard to his chest and there before whoever was looking, Adam kissed Florence until she found herself feeble and clinging to him. When he released her, she was weak in the knees, keeping her hand on his arm, but her eyes on the ground. "Don't ever do that again," she said, hoarsely.

"I will, Fleur. If the moment presents, I will. I'm asking you here and now, Fleur." He went down on one knee, "will you forget the past and marry me. Let us have a happy life together?"

"Get up. Get up." She glanced toward the Inn, frantic, beside herself. "Are you crazy?" He remained, one knee on the icy sidewalk. "Please, Adam, don't embarrass me or yourself."

Resolve blazed across his features. "Do you think I care, Fleur?" She was gripping his hand now, forcing him to rise before he fell sideways. "Think it over. I ask you to marry me."

Annoyed, she snapped, "help me get to the door, before I have a nervous break-down."

Laughing, Adam rose up, placing one hand to the hollow of her back and the other firmly holding her elbow. "I take that as you will think about it," he said, his laugher proceeding them up the path, to the door. "And, if anyone saw me kiss you, just tell them I love you and always have." He looked dangerously settled and ready to kiss her again. "And always will." Gallantly, he opened the door and bowed, "There you go my lady and I will see you tomorrow."

Chapter 10

She sailed past a young couple pushing a baby in a stroller down the hall, keyed the lock to her door and stepping inside, flung the long coat into the nearest chair, passed into the bathroom and was washing her hands hard enough to take the skin off when in the mirror, she saw Nancy Ann sitting on her bed. Flushed and embarrassed, with the towel in her hands she walked back into the bedroom's sitting area.

"I didn't see you."

"You weren't expecting to find me sitting on your bed? Deidre' let me in with my promise to be sure the door was locked when I left. I brought your scarf and gloves. You left them the other night. We have more weather on the way and you may need them."

Both were silent for a moment. "You saw that, didn't you?" Florence began. "I was in a stew."

"What's it all about?" Nancy Ann patted the bed covers beside her. "Sit. Tell me."

"It's Adam. The nerve of him."

"Deidre' thought you went off with a man in a truck. Her way of not telling me anything."

"Yes, it is all about her, too." Florence let her chin fall to her chest. "I sound like a spoiled accusing child, don't I?" She got a grip on herself and continued. "You may not know this, one of the young men, a guest here, told his dad who told me, Deidre' had planned an event and the weather canceled it out, leaving her with a large inventory of foods for the event she can not cancel out at this late date."

"She usually has an event either Labor Day or mid-November and once at Christmas as I recall. I attended a couple but mostly they were for the business between her and the nearest towns to keep an interest going of what is available along the interstate for travelers who like to shop."

"Yes, that's how I understand it, but this time she got caught with all the trappings, I mean food and as I understand at a hefty price. She's upset because she doesn't have money to pay, that was to be taken care of with the proceeds she makes from the event. Anyway, I agreed with Adam to figure out a way to continue the event but how are we to draw the people in."

"So, you and Adam put your heads together and what did you decide?"

"Why not make it a Harvest festival, make reservations available to the shop people of Mosby and the farmers along the route who sell pumpkins and apples and to the many lone artist who sell their product along the way..." She stopped explaining and waited for Nancy Ann's opinion. "Do you think it will work? Will the people of Mosby embrace the idea or scorn it?"

"Let's think about this. Did the people who have pumpkin patches and apple orchards have time to gather the fruit or harvest the pumpkins before the snow came in. This snow storm was earlier than most." She was quiet, thinking. "And Deidre' can go ahead with the event but it will be used as a gathering of the locals...hmmm, to create and encourage them in how they present their product. Right?" Florence nodded, "and help Deidre' not suffer financial loss."

"Yes." Florence stared at Nan. "Will it work?" She stood up to peer down on Nancy Ann.

"I don't know. It should. Why don't we canvas the downtown area shops tomorrow and see?" Florence was hugging her. "Don't get too excited, yet." Nan was smiling. "Now, why did you fling your coat in the chair and look like you wanted to run over someone with a bulldozer?"

"It was Adam. He did a conspicable thing." Nan's mouth flew open. "Yes, boy wonder," Florene agreed. "You think he's so perfect. I can tell. Well, he's not. He's a man like any other." Nan was waiting, an expression of unbelief on her face. "Oh, yes, you can shake your head if you want. We had this agreement, not to bring up our past relationship or I would not work with him on this project."

"You are killing me. What did he do?" Nan fairly shouted. "Our, Adam? Boy Wonder?"

Florene fell back on the bed. "I almost fell. When you leave remember the sidewalk is like glass, iced over. Anyway, when I was falling, I had no sense of grabbing on to anything. Nothing was there, except Adam and he caught me."

Nancy Ann was nodding. "Good for Adam. You could have broken something or got a knot on your head."

"Nooo," Florence no, sounded warning. "He kissed me. Caught me first, pulled me to his body and kissed me. I haven't been kissed in years." Florence was near hysterics.

Nan could hardly keep from laughing, but she saw seriousness was expected. "Adam kissed you?"

Indignantly, Florene replied, "He did. But that's not all."

"There's more?" Florene was nodding, violently. Nan reached over to smooth her hair.

"He asked me to marry him. Down on one knee right out there in front of God and anyone else that passed by, on that icy sidewalk, ask me to marry him. 'Marry, me, Fleur," he said, "and let's live a happy life together."

Nancy Ann fell back on the bed, laughing, her belly shaking like jelly, and she couldn't stop. Florene sit up and stared at her. "Is that all you can do? I was embarrassed, the nerve of him."

"Fleur, you are in shock. I'm a bit, myself. Boy Wonder has decided to stake his claim." She gulped to keep from going into laughter again, Florence looked ready to blow. "Fleur, don't be upset. Think about it. He does still love you. He can't control that love. He wants you to know."

"Too late." Florence expression was that of a child that had been wrong and would not accept an apology. "Twenty some years too late. He wed a woman he didn't even love and let her walk all over him."

"There must have been a reason, Fleur. We always thought there was more to the story than just saving the name of a wealthy girl from the city. In those days no one broadcast a pregnancy out of marriage. They hurried and covered it up, or left for awhile and came back empty handed."

"It wasn't right for him to do me that way."

"Fleur, you didn't talk bad about Adam when it happened. Why did you accept it and move on? I always wondered if there was more than the one night you said you and Adam shared when you promised never to contact each other. What is the rest of the story?"

"What do you mean? Were there other nights together? No. Never. Isn't it enough that he broke my heart, and maybe his in the process? Why am I supposed to be so forgiving now? I raised our son, alone." Her eyes filled with tears. "I don't owe him anything."

"Fleur, the question is, where did this uncontrolled anger come from? This isn't you, Fleur."

"I don't know." Florence took a deep breath as tears streamed down her cheeks. "Maybe this is the real me. Maybe I've been brittle all these years just waiting for the dam to break." She glanced to

Nancy Ann. "Do you know what he asked me? Was I so hard hearted and bitter I couldn't forgive? Maybe I can't."

Nan squeezed Florence hand. "You will, my friend. You are loving and kind. Just give it time."

"Nan, sometimes I just want to die. If I didn't have Matthew, life would be difficult."

"Why's that, Fleur?"

"Oh, Nan, when you were single, didn't you get tired of the endless responsibilities with no one helping you?" Fleur sighed. "Before I married, which was a mistake since he was a skirt chaser, even then I had my hands full, a single mother pushing a little boy in a stroller, loading it into the car, even filling the gas tank….you know….endless tasks. It makes me tired to think about it."

Nan pat Fleur's arm. "And look at us now, you just received a proposal, that by the way could change your life…and I, I have this happy hunk of man at home, waiting for me." She jumped up. "I'll be here about ten in the morning and we will stir up Mosby front and center." She was almost out the door when she turned back and said, "You might reconsider that proposal. You wouldn't have to fill up the vehicle by yourself." She wiggled her eyebrows and shut the door, then opened it again, "And there might be other benefits…like not being alone." Florence shoe hit the door and Nan went down the hall laughing.

* * * * *

True to her word, Nan arrived at the Inn mid-morning. Florence had finished helping Deidre' with the rush of morning breakfast and once it was evident Terence was in charge of clean-up, she was ready and waiting for Nancy driving up to the door in her dad's old truck.

"I thought we'd go in something the locals recognize. They'll remember you once we start mingling. "Get in." Florence was barely in the seat when Nan wheeled out the drive.

"Mercy, Nan, this thing is a spinner on wheels. Do you always take off that fast?"

"We have things to do. So, get that note book ready and a couple of pens to take notes."

The shops were just opening, windows displaying different arts and crafts. "Marge's shop will be on the list, but let's leave it until last. Marge is a bummer for helping with whatever comes along and I have a feeling we are going to need her."

Once they reached the small park adjacent to Center Square, Nancy parked the truck and they began walking. "What's our spiel?" She waited for Fleur to reply. "You know, what is it we want?" Fleur gawked at her. "Fleur, we have to have something made up to tell them our plan, a celebration among the shop folk, before the travelers on the road enter Mosby"

"You're the one with all the jive and grandiloquence."

"Grandiloquence?" Nan let the word role off her tongue. "So that's what it is? Hmmm. So, shall I begin and you will back me up." She grinned. "Here's Amy Moon's shop. Let's begin with her." The shop was quiet, when they entered, the door closed against the cold, but they could hear a noise coming from the back room. "That's Amy, back to us, concentrating, anyone could come in and steal her blind. She always concentrates."

"Hey, Amy." Amy came into the room, carrying a half dozen of the dolls she made.

After introduction and a viewing of Amy's soft bodied dolls, Nan launched into the reason for the visit and Florence jotted down Amy's suggestion and opinion of how the event might succeed. "That's what we need, Fleur. The shop owner's knowledge of what works and what doesn't." They left with their arms filled with Amy's dolls.

"Maybe you can find a way to use them in decorating the room," Amy suggested. "Good advertisement for me with the holidays approaching."

"I think we should stop in to Mr. Amos, next. What do you think?"

Florence raised eyebrows meant she remembered Mr. Amos. "You think?"

"Let's see if he makes the connection. He grows pumpkins now and we will know from him if the people were able to gather any produce before the early snowstorm." Nancy Ann slid into the old truck, stacked the dolls in between them and drove through the shop district. Mr. Amos pumpkin patch was still covered in snow, the remaining pumpkins visible as bumps under a blanket. "I don't know about this," Nan said, as they climbed out of the truck and walked a path to a small wooden shop with pumpkins cut out of wood lining the way.

"Attractive," Florence commented, as they pushed through the door to warmth and Mr. Amos, busy behind the counter, wiping down small pumpkins.

"So you were able to harvest a few before the snow came in," Nancy Ann said, in greeting.

Turning, Mr. Amos, said, "Ladies. How may I help you?" His accent as distinguish as always, a smile went across his face. "Nancy Ann, did you come back to buy a pumpkin or to see if there's any weeds left outside, safe from the snow?" He peered into Florence face, "and you, young lady, are you the one that was with her? The girl from the city that visited each summer?"

Florence extended a hand. "That's me. I came to apologize, again."

They all shared laughter, as he pointed to chairs centered around a pot-bellied stove. "Sit o'er there," he said. "It will refresh the stories you've heard of warming one side while the other side is cold, but the old stove lends atmosphere and some of the young ones have no idea how we used to heat our homes."

Florence glanced around. "Nostalgic, Sir. I can see you've made an addition to your work."

"It is work," he admitted, "and I'm getting old to it, but a couple more years, as we do have generous travelers who frequent our shops, off the Interstate, mind you, because here in our area, most of us grow our own."

"You are saying the shops here in Mosby supply items of use to those traveling the Interstate?" He was nodding. "Then, Mr. Amos, what do you think about the Inn? Is it needed in Mosby?"

"My opinion?" He pinned his eyes on Florence, "Funny you would ask. I've had a few inquiries concerning the Inn, lately, a questionnaire thing of sorts, how important is the Inn to this area, what would benefit travelers more, if it was improved or replaced and it made me wonder why someone would call me."

Florence found the information interesting. Leaning forward, she asked, "You mean complete strangers called you?"

"They did with a follow up of a paper questionnaire coming in the mail, soon after."

Nan interrupted, "I'm interested in your answers, Mr. Amos."

"Well, take this snow storm. Sometimes they come in unexpected, even the weather man is caught off guard and I think the Inn is an asset to our little community. Sometimes the travelers are weary and want a little rest before going over the mountains. That's a long stretch and," he smiled, "you know the ladies like to shop and that's what we've turned in to. Shops."

"Your opinion is the Inn should remain?"

Mr. Amos studied the question a moment before looking Florene in the eye. "My opinion and my wonder is why Galant hasn't done something with the Inn. It's outdated. He could have a real winner, there, if he'd quit running off on his exotic vacations. Deidre' does the best she can, but she doesn't have partnership in it, to bring it up to par. Fact, is, if someone doesn't do something, a year or two down the road the Inn will be like a sinking ship."

"We are here to see how you would feel about the community of Mosby joining in together, particularly those who bring in revenue, by selling to the interstate travelers," Nancy Ann, explained. "Just between you and us, Mr. Amos, Deidre' is in a bit of a quandary, due to this snow storm." She explained the circumstance. "But we won't be telling this to everyone."

Once back in the truck, Florence ask, "Is Deidre' a local girl?"

"I don't remember her from our day, but she's young, twenty-ish, so I wouldn't, but she has been trying to keep the Inn going for Galant the last five years. Joe, Elizabeth's boss, seems to help her out."

"And Joe, is the owner of the night club Deidre' sent me to, for bottled water. Right?"

Nancy Ann nodded, grinning, "and Catrin's husband. Remember, the pain Catrin put Elizabeth through? Over Eric, but he escaped to California, out of her reach and she found Joe."

"Who knew a small town, like Mosby, could have such drama?"

"I think, as long as there's three people, there could be drama if there's one different in gender, don't you? Two are going to find each other and that leaves one out."

"Painfully, you are right. I'm part of that equation. Or, I should say, I was."

Cautiously, Nan replied, gently, "It sounds like you have a new opportunity."

"Careful, friend, I don't have a shoe to throw at you, at the moment."

Nancy Ann sighed. "I know. You carry a lot of hurt but you did receive a wonderful gift from knowing Adam. What are the chances of your son and his father meeting here in Mosby?"

"I can't worry about that right now, Nan. Finding Adam here, was a shock to my system. I thought you had told me he moved to New York, and you did forget to tell me he and Charlotte were no longer together."

"It was my intention, not to stir up memories that were result of a sad time in your life."

"Memories are that, aren't they? They exist in spite of our trying to forget them."

"Tell me about it. I have T.J. as a reminder of Frank's affair, but you know what? It doesn't hurt half as bad that Frank betrayed me, since I have my dear sweet Jonathan." She took a deep breath, pulling into the Square's parking lot. "Let's get this walking tour of the shop owners over and head back to the Inn and do some plotting."

After visiting a number of owners, the two were quite weary when they climbed back in to the truck to head back to the Inn. "It was fun, having crackers and cheese with Marge, wasn't it? But you seem quite pensive, Fleur. What's going through your mind?"

"Marge and three others said they had received the same questionnaire Mr. Amos mentioned."

"And this bothers you, because?"

Florence shrugged. "It's all part of what we are working toward, isn't it? Whether our attempt to help Deidre' recoup finances out of her own pocket, due to an annual event she normally holds, that was blotted out by the unexpected snow storm?"

"Interest seems good and all are willing to purchase a reservation to the dinner. As Marge suggested, we need to make the event both educational and entertaining." Nancy Ann saw her friend's expression. "I know you, Fleur, there's more, but I won't push you. If you want me to know, you will tell me."

Florence reached across to lay her hand on top of Nan's on the steering wheel. "Thanks, Nan." It wasn't time to tell anyone why she was interested in the Inn. It might fall through.

"Shall we call Adam, or meet tomorrow? Marge said she might join us."

"I need to call Matthew. Let's make it tomorrow. Do you want to set up the time, with Adam?"

Nan grinned, "Save you from talking with him? Sure. I'm game." She began to laugh, "I can't wait until tomorrow to see how the two of you handle being together. I think I'll bring Jonathan along, in case pastoral assistance is needed."

"Ohhh," Florence groaned. "You never change." Closing the truck door, she said, "See you tomorrow."

* * * * *

"That's that." Nancy Ann settled onto the sofa with Jonathan. "Adam wants us to meet at his house. Are you up to joining us tomorrow? Adam's calling Bobby, that way he can work with the people, if there's need, for those who not only are shop owners but members of his church."

"I need to tell you, Bobby actually called this morning while you were away." Jonathan smiled, "I don't know if this is something you want, but the church has grown and his people think they need an assistant pastor, since it's obviously running Bobby ragged…trying to fill both capacities…and guess who they are thinking of calling?"

Their conversation was halted when Elizabeth and T.J. came through, all bustle and brass as Nan was wont to call them. Each held a sandwich and drink in hand. "We couldn't wait," Elizabeth explained. "It was so busy at the club we didn't have time for even a snack, and it is freezing out there, I bet we get more bad weather." She shivered. "Probably ice, this time."

"With the temperature dropping," T.J. added, "Joe decided to close when the last guest finished eating. We were swamped. It was like, no one wanted to stay home, tonight and then the weather changed and they finished eating and hurried home. He didn't think anyone else would face the cold," T.J. laughed, "but we did meet two vehicles going up the hill."

Nancy Ann glanced at Jonathan. "That would be all we need, to stop everything we have in the making of an event to help out Deidre' save finances and present Mosby in a way most around here haven't even thought of."

Elizabeth settled on the ottoman nearest the fireplace. "Tell me. I don't know what you are talking about." She listened while her mother explained the reason behind the event. "And where would you hold this sha-bang?" She saw her mother's expression. "Surely you were not thinking the event room at the Inn large enough?"

"What would we do, otherwise? Deidre' has to oversee the food preparation. That's what this is all about, her first event fell apart due to the weather, now we have the natives interested, probably because they all have cabin fever by now and want to get out...but it still remains the food has to be cooked and Deidre' has the equipment at the Inn."

"But there's not enough room to cater to say, five hundred plus people and should any of the business across the mountain think to join in, where will you put them?"

Nancy Ann, hid her face into Jonathan's shoulder. "Just hit her. She hasn't been here ten minutes and she's already pointing out possible problems."

"Or, she has something in mind," he replied, putting his arm around his wife and pulling her close.

"Well, we can't have it at the church." She said, "I know Bobby will suggest that, but there will probably be liquor served."

"That might be another problem," Jonathan grinned. "The pastor might learn a thing or two, about his people." He held his hands up, "Just saying, some don't like their minister knowing they imbibe." He watched Elizabeth holding her feet near the fire. "I think, your daughter might have an idea. Why don't you ask her?"

T.J. laughed as Elizabeth's phone rang and she left the room, saying, "It's Derek." When she returned thirty minutes later, her mother was asleep in Jonathan's arms and T.J. had gone to his room, upstairs. "I guess I should turn in, too."

"Everything all right with your young man?"

Elizabeth smiled at Jonathan. "Yes, thanks for asking. He is coming home next weekend and will start preparing for moving his business back to Mosby."

"Does that mean we will see you moving the date up for the wedding?"

"No, I think we will stick with a Christmas wedding. We began our love affair with plans to be married at Christmas and who knew it would take a year, once he began the process of moving his business from California? There were so many loose ends, we just kept putting it off, but now we don't have to any longer."

"It will be a happy occasion." Nan moved and he placed the Afghan around her shoulders. "It is rare, a couple can delay such an important moment, but you and Derek have."

"It is difficult having a relationship in two different states, Jonathan, but his business was flourishing and I had to return to my old position for three months, to train the new member to the firm, since I agreed when I left that I would, in order to keep an interest in the law firm," She sighed, "although I was no longer an active partner."

"When you became an employee at Fabrication, didn't they shake their head and say you were over skilled?" He grinned, "I mean, from a law office to being a book keeper."

It was her turn to smile. "I think my credentials are what gave me a good salary. You might say they had an in-home expert hired under the auspice of keeping books, but then the boss fired me." She laughed heartily. "And that's when I went up the hill, seeking employment, and met Joe. Little did I realize he was Catrin's husband. Talk about a crazy world. I go to work for Derek, not knowing he is the owner of Fabrication, and then I'm hired by Catrin's husband as a waitress in his club while his wife is off on one of her many times of living separate."

"Did she ever come in to the club, and make things a bit difficult for you?"

"Oh, yes, she rubbed my nose in her lady like ways many times. Believe me, Catrin is very ept." She started out of the room and stopped. "Some of the things that happened, seem trivial, now, but at the time, devastating." She yawned. "I enjoy talking with you, Jonathan."

"Same here, Ellizabeth." A new thought entered his mind. "Is Catrin with Joe, now?"

"No, she is in New York, living in her parent's home. Joe spends free time, playing cards with Adam." She paused on the first stair. "They are two lonely men, doing the best they can."

"I've been there, Elizabeth, when my wife died, I thought I'd sink, but in time the good Lord let your mother show up one Sunday morning in my congregation, and blessed me again."

"It's not easy, is it? When my husband finally found the one, he wanted to settle down with, and believe me it took him awhile, even while we were married, I was lonely. That's why I came back to Safe Haven. I thought Derek had moved far enough away I'd never run in to him. California seemed an impossible distance from Mosby." She laughed. "Doesn't God work in mysterious ways?"

"Yes, he does," Jonathan agreed. He listened to her footsteps on the stairs and when the door closed to her room, he said, "Nan. My darling. Wake up. Let's go to bed."

"Do we have to? This is so comfortable."

"Yes, my love. I'm getting a crick in my neck."

Nancy Ann moved, taking the Afghan with her. "I'm sorry, darling. I guess I talked too much today. Fleur got really quiet at times and I don't know what that was about." She started toward the bedroom. "Oh, no, I have to text and tell her we will be going to Adams tomorrow."

"How will she feel about that?"

Nancy Ann began to laugh. Picking up the cell, she text. "Meet us out front 10:30 in the morning. Goodnight, sleep tight."

"Can I sleep in my clothes?" Jonathan was plumping his pillow. She saw his expression. "Guess not." He had laid her gown on the end of the bed. "I might have some of Mr. Amos pumpkin stuff on me, anyway." She stripped down and slipped on the gown and climbed in beside him. Jonathan pulled her close.

"Nice. A good night kiss and I'll sleep like a princess."

"That snores," he agreed, a chuckle ending their nightly routine. "Good night, Princess."

* * * * *

Chapter 11

Terence found her on the way out. She keyed the door and turned as he called her name.

"Miss Florence, you want me to clean your room? I've not done anything for you, but look," he held his hand out for her inspection. "It looks good. I wanted you to see it before I did the re-wrap. Do you think I should keep wrapping it?"

She studied the cut. "As you said, it is healing very well, but yes, do keep it wrapped a few more days since you are into the cleaning products." She smiled and tousled his hair, "you are quite a nice young man, Terence, helping Deidre'. I don't think she could make it without you."

"Thanks to you," Terence grinned, "Dad actually helped those first few days and Mr. Adam did, too, one day. The one that was so hectic." Terence laughed. "You didn't know? He even ironed a few pillow cases. I did tease him pretty heavy though about sleeping on embroidered linens." He was watching her interest in mention of Mr. Adam. "I bet you do, too."

When she laughed, he said, "I thought so. You two would make a good pair, so precise about everything. I wasn't sure I could trust him with the Lavendar spray."

"Lavendar spray?"

"Yeah, you can ask him about that." He grinned, seeming to want to say more." She waited. "Well, I did see him kiss you and what was that knee thing he did? Was he asking your forgiveness or asking you to marry him?" She groaned. "Yeah, I saw. I told my dad and he said he'd like to kiss you, too." Terence shook his head. "Don't mess with my dad. He's not good husband material."

"Terence, I'm not looking for a husband, but what a thing to say about your dad."

He shrugged. "It's the truth." He stated down the hall. "I better wrap this hand. Deidre' has something for me to do, but remember Mr. Adam is a better catch than my dad any day."

"Terence." She smiled, as he waved and kept going. Glancing at her watch she thought it time for Nan and Jonathan. She wished Terence had not seen Adam kiss her and for sure not to have passed the info on to his dad. Sometimes she didn't know how to take Ray.

Speak of the devil, she thought, as she stepped outside the building. Ray was standing by the Jeep. "Hello, Beautiful Florence Nightingale."

"Morning, Ray."

"I was wondering if you would like to take a ride and see what this country looks like."

"Oh, Ray, thank you but I have an appointment. Maybe another day." For lack of knowing what to do, she slid in to the Jeep as Nan's old truck came into view. As though discussed, Nancy Ann and Jonathan came across and climbed into the back seat of the Jeep.

"Morning. Morning." She heard them address Ray, as she keyed the engine and backed away. "Something tells me that fellow would like to have come with us," Nan said quietly.

"Strange you would say that. Ray's son just warned me about him."

"Really? Do you want to enlarge on that statement?"

Meeting Nan's eyes by way of the visor mirror, Florence shook her head. "No."

* * * * *

"Adam said we are to let ourselves in." It was half a dozen steps up to the heavy stained door with ornate curved iron trim. Jonathan turned the handle and they walked into a foyer, neither Nan or Florence had seen before. "We always came in the back," Nan whispered, as a wafting fragrance promising good things, hit their senses with wild abandon. "Cinnamon," Nan said, her nose in the air like a Lab searching for game.

"Yeast rolls," Florence added. Jonathan stood staring at the two as though they had lost their minds. Both began to giggle, tucking each an arm into Jonathan's and heading into the house.

"Marge is here." Nan glanced up to her husband. "Before you ask, no one makes cinnamon yeast rolls like Marge. Trust me. They are to die for."

"For a minute, there, I thought the two of you had died and gone to heaven by the look on your faces. If just the smell and memory does that, I can't wait for the first bite."

They passed through the wide hall that led to the bedrooms and then to the open sitting room with its fireplace and painting, and on to the open kitchen and gathering room where Marge rose up to meet them, her arms open wide and a smile of welcome. "At last," she cried out. "You're here." Arms became tangled, heads on shoulders and a generous sound of laughter as the back door opened and Adam came in carrying an arm full of wood for the fireplace.

They watched as he applied several blocks, stacked the other on the hearth to one side and turned to them. "What a joyous wonderful sound, at last, to hear laughter in this house. Welcome and thank you for coming. Now, enjoy Marge's wonderful delicacy. I promise you will think you have died and gone to heaven and there's coffee, hot chocolate, or whatever you want…and then we can get down to business."

* * * * *

"Marge, you rival the best bakeries in France," Jonathan smiled. "How nice to meet you, at last." He explained, "my church took a youth group to France and they found the street that housed the most wonderful delicacies…and we went there every day after handing out pamphlets."

"Why France?"

"It was a time travel was restricted, we had a stop in France and since there are not that many denominational churches such as ours, we decided our youth could still minister to the population. They are fifty percent Catholic-Christian, true, but not everyone has been reached."

"And you rewarded yourselves with sweet sugar delicacies." Marge smiled. "Life often gives us opportunities of the most-simple nature. We think nothing of, at the time, but some where down the road what was simple pops up as a sweet memory and it was part of a lesson we needed." She took the chair opposite Jonathan. "Will you miss being an active minister?"

Jonathan glanced to where Nancy Ann and Florence were jotting down possible vendors that might be interested in helping with the event. "At least attending," he heard his wife say. After his wife died, trying to stay in the ministry, he had been a sinking ship until he met Nancy Ann. "I don't know how to answer that, Marge, life with Nan is good. There are seasons of life."

At that moment, Bobby Dugan came into the kitchen. "I heard that question and I hope Jonathan comes on board our church and helps us. Mosby is growing, after all these years. People like the laid-back atmosphere, which means more folks to contact. We can use Jonathan. We are just waiting on him to decide." Taking one of the rolls he hugged Marge, "Should my wife leave me, will you marry me? I could eat these rolls every day of my life."

Marge laughed, "you wouldn't last long." He was making the rounds, hugging Florence and Nancy Ann, tapping Adam on the shoulder.

"Gotta get after this old boy, haven't seen you in the pew, yet, Adam."

Adam grinned. "You think the roof wouldn't fall in?"

"What I think is, I'm inviting all of you for this coming Sunday. Let's fill the pews. Yeah, they'll think its part of your pushing this Event thing Deidre' will have and is, but it can't hurt." Bobby licked one finger where cinnamon had rest, rubbed his hands on the napkin Marge hand to him and said, "Let's get this show on the road, I have another appointment."

* * * * *

They were on the way home, Nancy Ann and Jonathan in the back seat, Florence driving.

"What am I? Your chauffeur?" Glancing at the two by way of the mirror, she laughed. "Oh, I get it, you are still honeymooners, holding hands. That's okay. I don't mind."

"How do you feel about the plans we've made? Bobby's a power house, isn't he? No change." Nancy Ann explained to Jonathan. "He was always where there was action.

"Or made it," Florence added. "At least he kept us focused. It was a good planning session, but I can see we will have to rely on each other for the unexpected, that will pop up."

"You didn't face Adam up on a few things I thought you would. I'm proud of you."

"Like our different opinion on whether to have entertainment?" Florene glanced back, "think about it, how do we work that in? The event will run late and where will they spend the night if the Inn is full?"

"I believe he offered to let them stay with him."

"Didn't we agree to keep it as tightly business as possible?" Florence sounded a bit petulant. "It's difficult knowing where to draw the line and not overstep in certain areas, such as privacy." She pulled into the Inn's drive, seeing Ray leaning against Nancy Ann's father's truck. "Hmmm." She said, aloud, wondering why he was out of the building. "You know, I would have thought since he missed the game with his son, that this fellow would have headed back home by now."

"Why does he look like he's a bit out of sorts?" Nancy Ann asked as Jonathan poked her. "Well," she said, "It's obvious. Did I park in his spot?"

Florence opened her door and stepped out. "Hey, Ray, what's going on that you're on the lot?"

He walked their way, addressing Florence question. "Deidre' tells me you met to discuss having an event to help her out." He took in Jonathan and Nancy Ann climbing from the back of the Jeep. "Wouldn't it have been a courteous act of kindness to include me in, since I'm the one told you about the whole thing?"

Florence was trying to grasp the significance of their conversation. "Ray, I had no idea this meant anything to you, and too, if I had thought there was reason to call on you, I probably would have dismissed it, thinking you and Terence would be heading back home."

"What do you know of our plans?" He asked, curtly. "We stopped in because we couldn't go over the mountain pass, and in this time, my son and I helped Deidre out of sheer kindness. Anyone can see she has her hands full."

Florence felt a flash of animosity toward Ray, but shook it down, quickly. Wasn't this the same grumpy man that first night? But in the next day he had earned forgiveness. She did a silent, apology for words she hadn't said, but thought. What kind of person was she, anyway?

"I'm sorry you felt left out. You have helped Deidre and Terence has been a God-send."

Jonathan stepped forward, extending a hand. "Ray, glad to meet you. I'm Jonathan and this is my wife, Nancy Ann." Stepping back, he continued, "I was just along for the ride, but these women, are the brain for the Event. I imagine they'll be glad to tell you the plans."

"Will you be here next week end, Ray?" Nancy Ann was sizing him up, even as she spoke.

"We aren't tied to any schedule. Yes, if that is the date you have set, we will stick around and maybe be of help in some way." Ray's demeanor was changing, the sulky look leaving his features. "Terence has taken a liking to Florence Nightingale, here." Ray smiled Florence's way.

* * * * *

"Yeah, yeah, yeah," Nancy Ann was driving the ruts like a race car driver on the way up the lane to Safe Haven. "Terence likes Florence Nightingale. If Fleur fell for someone like that Ray guy, I'd have to shoot her or him one."

"Is that a confession?" Jonathan gripped the dash as she hit a spot that caused the truck to rock through one side to the other. "Darling," he said, "Could you slow it down so we make the last two hundred yards to home? I feel like Marge's cinnamon rolls are going to up and out."

"For heaven's sakes, Jonathan, you are a minister. Surely you could see, he is a fake. Why is he still here? You heard why he was supposedly here, taking his son to a basket ball game? I find the distance more than any parent would travel."

"The boy may be suffering over loss of his mother, and if the Ray fellow as you call him, fell for Florence, what reason would you give that he should not try his luck?"

Jonathan listened as she mumbled. "He's a fake. There's a reason he's lingering and I'm going to get on the computer and search him out." She successfully braked and the truck came to a shivering stop. She didn't wait but bounced out the seat, hurrying up the path to the porch, leaving Jonathan wide eyed and chuckling. She was a pepper pot. To prove his thought, she called back, "Get that bag, will you, that Adam gave us as we left and hurry up. I don't want you falling on those icy steps. Move it Padre'."

An hour later, appearing crest fallen at best, she sank down beside him on the sofa in front of the fire. "I found his wife's obituary, one son, that would be Terence, and the city where they lived. But, if he is the same person, which I can't prove without more info, there is man, connected to a business I believe means instrumental in the closing of big business."

"Oh, and what title are you speaking, my darling?" Jonathan pulled her close. "I've been sitting here, waiting for you to finish Deidre's business deal, so you and I could discuss mine." He chuckled. "You are aware that Bobby is pushing hard for me to come on board your local church."

"Are you implying I am a busy body?"

"NO, my love you care about your friends, but I believe Florence will take care of herself."

"Really? Did you notice how she ignored Adam, completely? Like if he had the plague."

Jonathan chuckled, tightening his hold. "I think it worked." He knew she would hit him. "Poor Adam, he won't know what has hit him, but I must say he seems set on Florence."

* * * * *

Wearily, Florence sank onto the bed, kicking free of the leather ankle boots and staring at the taupe ankle pants that had fit together so well. She had seen approval of her appearance in Adam's eyes. How many times had he touched her, not that anyone else would notice, but she had. She also realized Nan was getting a full reading of her decision to ignore Adam as much as possible. Well, much as she loved Nan, it was not her decision to make. She had not had to raise a boy alone, twenty some years. At that, Florence fell back on the bed. Of course, not. Nan had raised a daughter and a son by another woman who took her husband. Florence sighed, heavily, remorseful, "I'm sorry, Nan," she whispered, closing her eyes and falling asleep.

She forced her eyes open. What was that sound? She needed a minute to decide where was she? Not home. But where was home? Wasn't she moving back to Mosby. Then it hit her. The cell was still in her purse. Why wasn't someone calling the house phone? But whose house. It hit her. She was at the Inn. Mosby Inn. She had fallen asleep. The drool on her cheek proved, she had gone into deep sleep. She scrambled to get off the bed, find her purse and found the phone on the last ring.

Breathless she said, "hello." Matthew's laugh held a bit of worry. "Mother?" She took a deep breath. "Yes, son, I must have fell asleep. One of those do before you die sleeps."

"Intriguing," he replied, his voice holding a trace of mystery. "You care to explain?"

"There's been a problem developed, concerning the Inn." She explained. "Long story short, some of us are trying to help the girl who runs the Inn when the owner is away."

Her son was laughing. "Mother, typical of you. Who will you help next?"

"Maybe, myself," she remarked, sounding a bit peevish. "Oh, Matthew, it makes me wonder if my last endeavor will be my worst."

"Kind of like rear up to bite you in the butt?" He asked.

"Exactly."

"You never fail, Mom." He reverted to the term of endearment he always slipped into when his heart was beating with hers and they were as they always said, "on the same page." She could feel the smile on his face. "Mom, you are the best. It will all work as you planned. I miss you." He waited for her reply. "Bye, Mom, I love you and it will, all, be all right."

She wished she felt better, but now her mind went into a spin reviewing the day's events. Being close to Adam had its effect. She was thankful he didn't remind her in front of everyone his words to her that day on the sidewalk. His words rang in her head. "I'm a man, Fleur. I'll do everything I can to win you over." She had to be on guard. No doubt, today was his test run to see if he could get under her skin. Why had she felt his presence, even when he was twelve feet across the room and she raised her eyes to see his on her?

What was with Ray? Waiting for her by Nan's truck, as if he was privy to her whereabouts and the nerve to imply, he should have been part of the group to decide about the event? Well, that was settled and she had explained, Deidre feeling confident in preparing the food in the confines of the Inn. "We will make a way," she told the group, "After the meal is served, tables will be moved, opening up the floor, for possible dancing." She had glanced to Marge, "You mentioned if we had the ensemble, there would be those wanting to dance, because Mosby seldom presents the opportunity." Bobby had been in charge of opening and closing the discussion, but when it came to the schedule of events, he had turned it over to Florence.

She asked, "Bobby, you mentioned the ensemble are part of your church, how is that going to affect them if there's liquor served and dancing?"

Bobby had paused from his usual spontaneous way of speaking. "I'm going to tell you. They live between Mosby and the larger cities to the East and West of us and they worship regularly with us. They are employed by Three Winds Resort. I was invited to attend and what they are capable of, is more than a small place in the middle of the road, like Mosby, would draw." He turned to Jonathan. "Tell me, Pastor, would you keep a group like that from joining your membership and adding beauty to Sunday worship service?" He closed his eyes waiting for Jonathan's reply as he added, "You must hear them play Amazing Grace."

Jonathan considered for a moment. "Would I judge their place of work, Bobby, are you asking that or, should I judge and have a say in whether they share the talent God gave them to add to the church worship on Sunday?" In a gentle voice, Jonathan said, "Shouldn't we let God decide?" As she thought about Jonathan's reply, Florence smiled. Nancy Ann had a good man.

Still, she didn't know what to make of Ray. He had raised a good kid, in Terence. He couldn't be all bad. Adam's words came to her; "Fleur, don't we all have something we hold dear to our heart, that no one else knows?" And she whispered, again, as on that day. "Yes, I suppose we do." But there was something about Ray, she had not figured out. He was up to something.

If, as they concluded every aspect to the Event was settled, why had Nancy Ann piped up on the last, "I suggest Fleur and Adam make a reservation for dinner at the Resort and check out the Ensemble." Florence shook her head as if to clear the cobwebs wrought by her ambitious friend. No, Nancy Ann hadn't changed, still trying to make things happen. She was thankful Adam had seemed not to hear and no outing was expected.

When her stomach growled, she considered if Deidre' would have left overs and then she remembered. Adam had given them a bag as they left; Marge, Bobby, Jonathan and Nan and herself, and now she was curious, why would he do such a thing? He had been a wonderful host, finger food and a plate of delicacies to make a sandwich as they planned had been unexpected. Neither she nor Nan had considered taking food, but Marge had supplied the delicious cinnamon rolls for which she was famous. Now, as she stared into the bag she saw the makings of a snack, and in between a package of specialty crackers, a note.

I love you Fleur. You looked beautiful today I will contact you about our reservations to the Three Winds Resort. Have a restful night. Adam

Stunned, she stumbled over to the small round table with two chairs and sit down to process what she had just read. Inside the bag, along with the crackers, she found a bottle of water, a small roll of summer sausage and an equal size roll of cheese. What kind of man did such a thing?

She had difficulty sleeping until somewhere between four and five o'clock in the morning she saw the first light across the mountains and sinking onto the bed closed her eyes. Hadn't she relived every moment of youth spent with Adam? Why? She had no plan to restart friendship or relationship with him. Her body was as exhausted as her mind, and unintentionally closing her eyes brought the magic of sleep. She had not set the alarm to waken, and only the sudden thud of something hitting the wall outside her door brought her from a deep sleep to face the clock with the hands pointing to nine o'clock.

Taking a deep breath, she realized breakfast hour had come and gone without her. As her eyes swept the room, she saw a small white envelope had been shoved under the door. Why would Deidre' be billing her when she knew she was staying for the event? Rising, still dressed in the taupe slacks and angora sweater from the day before, she went to the door and picked up the envelope.

Tonight. Wear something festive or night clubbish. Reservation at Three Winds Resort. I'll pick you up at six. Dinner will be served at seven and dancing thereafter. Adam

Just like that, he thought he could sweep her off her feet.

Chapter 12

She reviewed the shock of the morning; Adam's note slipped under the door. Reservations to Three Winds Resort to view the Ensemble. Thinking she was perfectly normal she made the bed, scrunched up the bag he had supplied the previous day, on second thought knowing breakfast hour was over, she retrieved the few remaining crackers, sliced the roll of sausage and cheese and sit munching, at the small table contemplating whether to reply to Adam's note.

How had he managed to have it delivered to her door? But, then, Terrence and Deidre' were his friends. She took a deep breath. Should she go? Go check out the wind ensemble? At Three Winds Resort? Another deep sigh and she went to the closet to view the meager wardrobe she had brought from New York. Sadly, she viewed herself in the mirror. Her hair was in need of a shampoo, her nails were splitting from the cold and she felt she was betraying her inner self if she went with Adam. Hadn't she resolved to punish him for all the years of hurt?

Why must the good side of her kick in and extol his merits. He didn't deserve a word of kindness. She was ashamed. "Are you so bitter and hard-hearted you won't give us a second chance?" Adam's words tormented her. All the years she remembered his gentle kind ways to find he hadn't changed, except he married another, and left her to fend for herself, after all the plans they had made. Maybe she was turning into his description, maybe now she was bitter and hard hearted. She procrastinated until past noon, neither opening her door to go down to the main room where she knew a dozen people would be stirring, Ray and Deidre' among them.

At two o'clock, Nancy Ann called. "Want to come for dinner tonight?"

"No, but thank you. I'm working on something. If it's okay, I'll see you tomorrow."

"All right, Fleur. Have a great day." Nan didn't do the usual cajoling. She was relieved.

Three o'clock arrived as she stepped into the shower; shampooing her hair, applied a gentle fragrance conditioner and slipping into a heavy terry robe, set about filing her nails to finish buffing them, and add a base of clear coat polish. Searching through the suitcase she found the solid pearl on a silver chain and the small pearl earrings that would match the beads on the one shoulder navy dress that fell to mid-calf. She hoped she had brought the matching suede heels.

By four thirty, she was pacing the floor, wondering if she should change her mind and send Adam a refusal. Instead, she sit down to try to calm her nerves and went to sleep in the chair. Had dinner not been served as usual between the five thirty and six thirty hour, she might have slept through, but the noise of early arrivers in the hall awakened her and with a start she jumped up to apply make-up, jewelry and comb her hair in to place before slipping into the navy dress. The nap had flushed her cheeks and widened her eyes. Even she had to admit, for a woman having had a sleepless night, she looked strangely alluring. Alluring. She laughed at her own description. Glancing at her reflection in the mirror, she whispered, "Betrayer."

Ten minutes to six, she gathered the only appropriate wrap she had to go with the navy off shoulder dress. Fake, white fox, she laughed at her reflection in the mirror. No one would know it was fake. "Looking good, girl," she whispered and walked out of the

room and closed the door. Not wishing to stir up opinions concerning where she was going, she left by the side door and walked to the
Jeep, ready to wait for Adam when she heard wheels on the ice.

"Great timing," he said, "I'm just a few early." Offering a hand,
he added, "You weren't ditching me, were you?" He motioned toward
the Jeep, as he opened the door, and held her hand as she got in the
truck. "Hope you don't mind, but it's essential to travel four-wheel
drive, here, through the winter months." He closed the door and
hurried around to the driver's side. "Umm, you smell heavenly, what
is that? You always wore Sensation or Nude. This is?"

"Nude," she replied softly. "I'm surprised you remember."

"I remember everything about you, Fleur." He chuckled. "I
remember your mother said the very name of the perfume meant it
was too old a fragrance for you, and she gave you a bottle of what
was it?"

"Vanilla Fields, which was lovely," Florence replied, remembering her mother blamed Nan's mother, "that the girls were enjoying
too much freedom, and she better clamp down on them."

"As I recall, she took the first bottle of cologne and you and
Nancy Ann saved money and purchased another bottle of..."

"Nude," Florence added, "and on the side, my mother was
enjoying the original and Nancy Ann's mother was laughing about
the whole thing. She was a wonderful auntie."

Silence ruled for a bit, when he asked, "How was your day?"

She gave an embarrassed laugh. "I spent most of it trying to
think why I should not come with you, tonight." He appeared hurt.
"Never mind, the act. You see where I am. Right?"

His grin was rewarding. "I'm glad you came with me, all in view
of Deidre's Event. Right?"

"Exactly."

A sprinkling of snow was beginning as they arrived at Three Winds. The Event Palace was front and center to arrival. Many couples appeared to enjoy the heated pool while snowflakes fell on the water. "I couldn't do it," she said in a low voice. "Maybe that is a figment."

"How you all doing?" He called out, dispelling any myth of, "maybe it wasn't so."

The outside was elegant but for all the elegance, the inside was more of a forty's reminder, with low hanging chandeliers over the white clothed tables, as the silverware gleamed by each place setting. "All black and white and sepia," he murmured. "I like it. What do you think?"

"It's nice," she replied as he pulled out the chair and she settled in. "Makes me think of the Stardust in New York, before they renovated. I kind of miss the glamour."

"Nostalgic," he agreed, placing his long coat on an empty chair. "Shall we decide what we'll order, in case the snow becomes a problem, and we have to leave quicker than we intended." He glanced around, "I think we arrived before the one who checks coats or the Matre'd made it to their station."

At that moment their person arrived to take order of their drinks. It was precisely seven o'clock and the ensemble was coming from one of the side doors to take places at a pre-arranged setting of their instruments. "Ah," Adam murmured, "Three-stringed, three-wind and a harp." He gave Florence a questioning glance. "Are they the one for Deidre's event?"

Florence was a bit skeptical, until she heard them, but she did wonder if Bobby was a little off base with this group. It was then another member joined the group, taking his place at a keyboard. The diners around the room began to clap, as he set the rhythm.

Fast paced, music surrounded them. Florence was so enraptured she didn't know their waiter came back to the table.

"Wow." Florence and Adam were clapping with the crowd. "Evidently," Florence said, motioning with one hand toward the neighboring tables, "they knew what to expect. When he joined them, they became a full class orchestra. Now, I see Bobby knows what he's talking about."

"Sounds like a full row of drums, doesn't it, and the harp, I could not imagine how it would all fit together. He is very talented and they are all accomplished musicians, aren't they?" People were leaving tables for the dance floor. "Would you care to dance? Our waiter said it will be at least thirty minutes, for our food to arrive, as the snow has brought more people in off the Interstate and the cook has a lot going on in the kitchen."

He was already standing, as she left the fox stole on the back of her chair and lay the small jeweled bag on the table and rose to take his hand. He did not pull her too close, but glanced down to meet her eyes, as they stepped in time to the Ensemble playing an oldie from their younger days. "Time goes by, so slowly," Adam sang into her ear. "Remember the year you stayed with your aunt and went to school at Mosby and we went to the dance that opened up Basketball season?" Florence closed her eyes, as if doing so would drown out his words. "I remember, you wore a skirt that had yards of material in it and when you sit down after we danced, the yardage draped the chair and lay on the floor, and you were not really comfortable."

The band went into a faster rhythm and they were both amazed to think they could keep pace. When the song ended, Adam led her back to the table. "I think we have realized this little Ensemble is more like an orchestra except for size, the volume and substance these people produce will surely be enough for Deidre's event." Once, they were seated, he said, "That was fun, Florence. We dance well together. If you would allow it, we could experience some nice evenings together."

Their waiter arrived with dinner and Florence was spared going over the agreement again. They ate in silence, but Florence was glad it was a comfortable silence. Once, Adam remarked, "the snow is gaining momentum, I'm thinking as wonderful as it was to hold you in my arms and dance with you, after all these years, we should start our little trip back to Mosby."

Once their attention was drawn to a group of teenagers laughing about the snow and their expression, of hot rodding it home, came to their ears, which made the two share raised eyebrows and Adam remarked, "I would shudder to think I had a child out in this snow tonight." Catching Florence glance, to the four going out on to the parking lot, he said, "you have almost a motherly expression on your face, for those kids, Fleur. Did you, by chance have children?"

A snow ball hit the window and the owner was making a hasty effort to go out to the teens, Florence avoided replying and hoped Adam forgot the question. It was their time to leave.

Taking note, the stole covered very little of her dress, Adam removed a pair of leather gloves from the pocket of his long coat before placing it around her shoulders, to her protest she would be all right. "I have this wool sport coat; I don't really need it." They hurried out into the night to find the parking lot covered in a possible inch or two of snow. "Thank God, for four-wheel drive," he said, as he helped her into the cab and then with a gloved hand swiped across the passenger side wind shield and went around to do to the same on the driver's side before he got in.

"Are you cold? I hate to be wearing your coat and you freezing. I'm afraid I didn't listen to the weather channel before dressing this afternoon." She glanced his way, seeing mainly the dash lit up casting a beam of light across his features. He seemed intent on driving carefully.

"No, I'm fine. You know how wool is. It's great if you need it and miserable if you don't." He glanced her way. "I haven't forgotten how wistful you were gazing at those teenagers." She didn't turn to him, but stared ahead. "I was wondering if you had children, Fleur? It's a bittersweet question. Of course, that was in our plans, wasn't it? To have one or two, hopefully a boy and a girl." She wouldn't turn her head. She sat staring straight ahead. "Did you have children, Fleur?"

At that moment, a girl popped up out of the road side ditch. Florence screamed. "It's one of them. The girl from the Three Winds. Where are the other three?"

Resolute, Adam sighed. "Where is their vehicle?" He was pulling to the side of the road, putting the vehicle in park and applying the emergency brake. He called out, "Where's your friends?" In the beam of the headlights, he saw the girl point downward. "They are in the ditch?" She was nodding and crying at the same time. "Are they hurt?"

Adam understood now. The vehicle was not down in the ditch as he feared. It had slid from right lane to emergency pull-off. Now, covered in snow it was almost invisible. The girl was as close to him as his shadow. "Did he brake hard and the vehicle went sliding out of control?" She nodded. He smiled. "Don't worry. It will be all right. Let me get a chain from my truck and we will pull it out."

"His Daddy's gonna be mad," she said, importantly. "He drives too fast, all the time."

"And you are?" Adam asked, slowing his walk back to the truck.

"His sister." Adam almost lost it. Instead, he grinned and said, "We'll get him out. What's his name?" Adam found the chain, and started back. She walked with him. Once they arrived at the truck. Adam knocked on the window. The boy and girl inside moved apart.

"George, Jr., seeing as you were the one braked hard because you were driving too fast on an iced pavement, how about, you climb out and offer your services." Adam saw the hesitation. "Or, if you prefer, you can sit in there where it's warm and we will call your father to come help you." The boy opened the door and slid out, the drop to the ground a bit more than he expected with the truck leaning. The girl followed. "Wasn't there another of you?" Georgie shook his head, while his sister piped up, quite helpful.

"We dropped him off, all ready. He has curfew."

"Shut up, Annabelle, you need to stay out of my business."

"I'm not in your business, Georgie. This is Daddy's truck. I doubt you get your own, now."

"All right, George, Jr. I'm going to show you where to hook a chain to keep from pulling the bumper off your truck." There was no response from George Jr. "Where would you put it?"

"I'd wrap that sucker around and around that bumper and jerk 'er right onto the road."

Adam slid down the iced ditch. "Man, we feel the thermostat dropping fast, now. Okay, it's here, and we have to have it attached properly or it will pull right loose. I'll do one side and you do the other. Then, you get behind the steering wheel, keep the motor running, and as I pull forward, you do the same. Keep your foot off the brake until it's time to stop on the pavement. Do you understand? Repeat the instructions, to me." Adam climbed back to the pavement.

Georgie got in the truck. "Whatta, I do, first?"

"We just discussed this. You tell me what you are going to do."

"Don't turn off motor. Put the truck in gear and go forward slowly til we're outta the ditch. Stop before I run into you, and then, me and Kristy will pick up where we left off."

"Did you forget to remove the chain, George Jr?" Adam eyed him through squinched eyes. "I believe you need to re-think how this happened and see that it doesn't happen again. No hot rodding on snow, no fast stops, everything thought out. That's what grown up young men do, not what some hot-headed child might do that is not ready to be driving the highway, yet."

George, Jr. started to defend himself, but decided better. "All right. I'll remove the chains once we're on level ground." He hesitated and then said, "Can Kristy ride with me."

Adam replied. "You are doing better, already, George Junior, but not great." Now he addressed the girls. "Annabelle, for safety's sake, you and Kristy, go get in the back seat of my truck."

Florence was silent as the girls climbed into the truck. "Girls, this is Miss Florence." She heard two meek replies of hello and then Adam was at the wheel of the truck.

The vehicle moved forward, slowly. There was a bilking sound of metal against snow, chain it's full length and George Junior's vehicle moved behind Adam's truck until it was on the highway. "Girl's stay put until Georgie and I unhook the chains and know his vehicle is running right." Adam took a deep breath, "Do either of you know if George Junior called his parents?" He heard Annabelle giggle.

"He didn't. You forget, I'm his sister. Dad would be mad as all get out." She seemed to reflect a moment. "I guess Georgie would have let us set there all night, if you hadn't come along."

Shaking his head, Adam glanced to Florence and closed the truck door. A few minutes later he was back. "Girl's walk carefully and join George Junior. You are going home. He promised." Taking a small card from his wallet, he handed it to Annabelle. "If your father wants to talk to me, this is my number. Shortly, they watched Georgie pass by, honking and waving like the teenage boy he was. Adam blew out a deep breath. "That wild boy needs a strong hand."

"You were never a wild boy."

"I wanted to be." He put the truck in gear and pulled onto the highway. "When I knew, you were gone to me. I wanted to go against every boundary ever set for me, defy the world."

"But you didn't," she said, quietly. "You settled down to accept responsibility that wasn't yours."

"Yes, I did." He sighed, resignedly. "Losing you, was the hardest thing in my life, then and now." He turned his eyes away from the road, for a minute. "We can't let that happen again."

"Thank you for a nice evening," She gave a small laugh. "That was at the Three Winds, what happened in the last hour has been enlightening."

"How, so?"

"It shows the kind of father you would have been."

Bitterness appeared in his reply. "I never had the chance."

She felt his pain and for a moment, she had her own, but then the old feelings stirred.

Chapter 13

"This is it." Bobby's voice boomed with excitement. "Today we begin preparation for an Event six days away! We have planned and prayed and now we get to work. I have a few members interested in helping, if we need them. How about you, Padre?" Bobby's interest in Jonathan never waned. "Made any decision about coming over to our church?" He gave a boisterous laugh. "All right, you don't want to commit, just now. Moving on. Nan has the list of people donating goods they want shown to the people over the mountain. Let's pray there's no further weather and the people over the mountain can get here."

Deidre entered to join the meeting, taking a seat by Adam. "Our Princess arrives," Bobby announced, "And we see you won the battle to prepare the meal for the event here, in your familiar surroundings. Good for you. I stayed out of that one." He and Deidre' shared a smile. "Florence, you and Adam checked out the Ensemble and approved. Is that correct?" Bobby saw Nan poke Florence in the ribs. "You two, will be teenagers at heart when you are a hundred."

There was a lull. Everyone locked in to their own thoughts. Finally, Bobby said, "Let's get started. Nan, tell us what we need to as far as serious attempts to win the business of the people over the mountain and the travelers on the highway as they pass by our little town of Mosby and Mosby Inn, the very feature and reason we are holding Deidre's Event."

No one seemed to notice, Nan's daughter, Elizabeth had joined the meeting, along with her boss. She and Joe, stood at the back of the room. She had listened to her mother and Jonathan going over a list of what must be done, in order to clear the room of the tables after the dinner was served, in order to continue with the entertainment. The whole thing bothered her and in that concern, she had discussed it with Joe. "I don't see how they can successfully dispose of tables that are not of the folding kind, but real set down and eat tables, sturdy and sizeable."

Joe had listened and ever ready to be assisting to Deidre's need, was now present and listening to the plans for the Event. He was waiting for Bobby to ask if there was any further business needed discussion. It was now, his moment. "Excuse me," he said, stepping forward.

"Have you considered, adding a bit of romantic flair to this Event? A ride complete with all the pomp to another location, where the music flows, the dance floor is clear and romance is in the air?" he turned to Elizabeth. "Your turn. Step forward and tell them what we have learned."

"Jud Arlin," Elizabeth began, "has felt a bit left out that no one visited his stables, thought to include him in this affair and he has offered the use of his men, who are well trained in handling the horse and buggys needed to pull off such a feat."

Everyone was leaning forward, listening. "This is a new twist," Bobby replied. "Explain."

"In the time, you spend, clearing the room of tables in order to stay at the Inn, you could load the people into the buggy's and deliver them to Joe's establishment, which he has offered free of charge. The atmosphere of elegance and a special occasion can be continued with the Ensemble set up there, and would end the Event with just the right amount of drama. They won't forget it." Elizabeth grinned, "and I think their hearts will commit to helping Mosby as a community fulfill its goal of becoming known for it's tradesmen, who do a fine job of producing quality items, whether sterling jewelry or Amy Moon's little baby dolls for the children, or Jud's fine horse and buggy rides."

"We all win," Joe continued. "I could use a little boost as far as people knowing I'm here. If it has entered any of your minds, to make Mosby more than a spot in the road before crossing the mountains, there's a reason so many of our craftsmen have relocated to Mosby. It has great potential to becoming a place, not like Gatlinburg or Branson, we don't have that many musicians, what we have are down to earth talented people trying to make a dollar in order to stay here in a perfect setting. What we need, is not just a perfect Inn to spend a night or a week, but along with the Inn capabilities, an atmosphere of this being a special spot on the earth and people go home to tell their friends and our success as a community continues."

Everyone was clapping hands as Bobby said, "Well done, my friend, you just put us on the map, but we do have eight fine musicians and I have a feeling if we pull this off, more will appear."

Within the next thirty minutes, an agreement was made. Jonathan, Bobby and Adam would speak with Jud Arlin, and make the decision whether to take Joe's offer of his establishment. Unknown to everyone, an uninvited guest lingered in the next room, listening to their plans.

As expected, there was a rash of reservations made. The advertising on radio and media was paying off. On Wednesday, in the line of usual business, eighteen people arrived at dusk, needing rooms before they went over the mountain for a two-day conference. All were praying weather didn't set in and keep them stranded and unable to return home for the weekend. Deidre' thinking of her own schedule prayed silently with them, please Lord, let the weather be good for our Event and she never lost sight, it was the people began the endeavor to keep her from going further in debt over the Inn.

Florence went down on Thursday morning to help Deidre prepare breakfast and found Ray and Terece, also, waiting to help. Terence was his usual young expressive self, however, his father was surly and resentful it seemed as he said, "I see you are busy, Florence Nightingale, making plans without any regard to my joining the fun." Taken aback, Florence merely stared at him, thinking to take it up later, but he persist. "For all the help and hope you give our Deidre,' surely you know the Inn is up for sale. What good will your precious event do for her then?"

"What?" his words caught her off guard. "You know the Inn is being sold?"

"It's public knowledge, except no one thought to tell her," He replied, pointing to Deidre.'

Stunned, Florence kept the news of his knowing to herself, but once the dishes were cleared and the kitchen in order, she went to her room and called Matthew. He was not available. She left a message. She tried to call Marge and got a message, saying, "I'm sick. Leave me alone."

Nan called. "I'm wondering, in the midst of all this hub-a-loo, do you have an idea what you will be wearing for the Event?" She listened as Florence replied, "I only have one dress, with me and, unfortunately I wore it to the Three Winds with Adam." To which Nancy Ann replied, "Remember how we could wear the same, except I'm shorter and the length was off on me? Come on over and let me show you a dress I've never worn, but would be perfect for you."

* * * * *

"How are things really going?" Nan asked as Florence followed her to the bedroom.

"Okay, I guess. It seems our plans are taking place. "All we can do is hope." She sighed. "If the little things would take care of their selves, like that Ray fellow. His son is terrific. The mother must have been remarkable to raise a good kid like that with a shifty daddy."

"It will be all right," Nan nodded, pointing to the dress. "I think the color will be good on you. Dark green is in, this season, and this one is so deep in color I think will appear almost black when the lights are low." She sighed. "I loved it, but the length doesn't show ankle length on me, it touches the floor and I hate to lose all that work at the bottom by cutting it off."

"Love it," Florence was smiling. "You are the best, thinking of me. Let me try it on."

"I'll leave you a minute, as there's a message on the phone I jotted down and left in the kitchen, it's about the Inn." She disappeared, leaving Florence unzipping the dress. When she returned, with paper in hand, Florence was admiring herself in front of the long mirror. "Wow, girl, you look fantastic. I knew you could do for that dress what I could not." They smiled. "Let me read this to you. "Dear Mrs. I understand you are a resident of Mosby. Your name passed to me by way of your past husband's old law firm. We are interested in knowing if the sale of Mosby Inn has transpired or is in the making. I'll leave you, requesting, please a call from you."

By way of the mirror, Florece stared back at her friend. "So, it is true, the Inn being sold has been made public. Just this morning, Ray asks me what Deidre's Event to bring awareness to people outside the community would mean once people realized the Inn was for sale."

"That was nervy. What business is it of his? Why is he staying on, I thought he had a home to go to."

"He does rub my thoughts the wrong way. There's just something abrasive about him. But in all fairness, I think he is at loose ends with losing his wife. I know Terence suffers her loss."

"You have empathy for him, my friend?" Nan peered at her with wise eyes. "But you can't forgive Adam?" She saw Florence stiffen. "I wouldn't tread dangerous ground bringing Adam up, if I didn't love you."

"I don't even understand it. I should never have come back to Mosby, but all these years it was as though something was left undone and I have to tie the pieces together before I die."

"How do I forgive him, Nan? Twenty some years of living with the fact he rejected me after we made all those plans? Now, he says he was never happy, I don't know if its true, he says they never consummated the marriage. She always had her baby's daddy in their life. Always."

"What does your heart say?" Nan sighed, sitting on the edge of the bed. "When you are with him, are you drawn to him, at all?"

Stooping, Florence let Nan unzip the dress and laying it behind Nan on the bed, slipped back into the tunic she wore over tight leggings. "Funny, you ask, I know what he is going to do or say, before he does it. It's as though nothing has changed; except I think he should pay for such an act; abandoning me for a woman he didn't even know."

"Fleur, don't you think he suffered? If she was not a wife to him, he existed in a world he had no part in making. Perhaps he loved the child, because Adam would. But there was nothing for him but despair in losing you. Who knows why it happened. Some say, in some weird way to protect his parents. What were they? Part of the Mafia?" She caught Florence expression. "Were they?" Her face lit up in astonishment. "You mean they were in danger and he had to marry the daughter to protect his parents? Unbelievable. No, you don't have to explain. That tid-bit made it's rounds but we all said it was drama to cover the real reason."

They were quiet for a minute, but Nancy Ann's mind moved on. "So, what about this Ray guy? Is he part of the Mafia, too?" They chuckled together. "Oh, Lord, help us. We aren't any bettor solving problems now, than we were then. Of course he's not. He's just a nervy lone wolf."

"Sometimes, I just want to let go and believe in all things good, Nan. But I have all this junk riding on my shoulders, years of questions of what could have been? It's hard to lose all the junk when it's been in your mind that long."

"Did you dwell on it every day, Fleur?"

"No, God was my strength, but being back in Mosby and running into Adam, it returned."

"Fleur, what if God brought both of you back at same time to give you a second chance?"

* * * * *

The morning of the Event, Florence rose early. She tried to reach Matthew but was told the Internet was down, possibly due to human error. It was thought another country was trying to intercept and destroy communication between large cities and in trying to protect an inexperienced operator had pressed the wrong button.

"Sounds like something I would do," Florence murmured. Slipping on her shoes, she glanced at the pedicure she had given herself. "Not bad, "Fleur," she said out loud. "Lord, girl, you need to get a life, talking to yourself." She had not known where to go, therefore did the job herself as she would be wearing strap sandals with most of her foot exposed. Nancy Ann had almost forgot to tell her there were matching shoes to the dress if they fit. Sandals had fit, if they had been enclosed shoes, she doubt her luck would have held. "Luck," she whispered, closing the door to her room. "If I'm lucky, the day will go well."

Ray was waiting outside the great room where other diners lingered over coffee. "I didn't know if you would come this morning," he said by way of greeting. "Big day, I suppose for Deidre's Event." Florence nodded, wondering where he was going with the remarks. At that moment Terence appeared. "I should tell you goodbye, Miss Florence. Dad says…" Terence words came to a halt. Florence had seen Ray shake his head as if to stop his son, speaking.

"Will you leave us, soon?" She asked, looking at Ray. Terence face was flushed red and anger was in his eye. It was between father and son, she was thinking, as she waited for Ray's reply.

"We did discuss it. If we are invited to tonight's shindig, we will wait until tomorrow. What do you think? Would we be welcome?"

"Anyone that's willing to purchase, is welcome, Ray." There was no other way to say it, the event was a fundraiser and he already knew that. She watched with heavy heart as Terence seemed to slink toward the door, avoiding a hearty how are ya from other people who seemed not only aware of his presence but found the teen very enterprising. It would be good if he had an enjoyable time at the event. What could she say to encourage him?

"Terence." She put out a hand to touch him, but he was pushing away. "I'll miss you," she said lamely. Ray was laughing and she cast a puzzled stare on the man. "Don't you feel his pain?"

Ray threw his hands up in the air. "And I can do something about it? Who do you think I am?"

"I'm surprised you are still here." She heard her own words, before realizing she had not meant to say them. Confused at the sudden anger she felt toward Terence's father, she turned away, but not before hearing him counter her words.

"Really? Then honey, stick around. Sometimes, life is enlightening. My boy has to grow up."

At three that afternoon, when Florence and Adam were left alone, Nan and Jonathan and Bobby had left, promising to return by six o'clock as the festivities would begin at seven. A mute Terence appeared to hand her a sheet of paper with a list of late attendee's names. "Thank you, Terence." Terence didn't reply. He just turned and walked away.

"What's with him? He usually gives me a hard time, but today, he has been in a funk."

"I'm sorry for him. I know his dad loves him, but I'm not sure he tries to understand him." She was studying the names. Ray's name was on the list, but not Terence. She felt sure Deidre' would have made a place for Terence. "His dad's name is on the list."

Adam wore a serious expression. "Are you two," he stalled for a moment, "great friends?"

"Not really, why?"

"Because I don't trust him. There's something fishy about why he's here. The kid can't help who his father is." He sighed. "I'd say his mother was exceptional to put up with Ray and at the same time give such good teaching to the kid. Mother's make all the difference." For a minute, she wanted to say, "you would have been a good father," but she didn't. Instead, she said, "I think I'll go, now. Deidre' has knocked herself out. The food smells heavenly and she does have girls to do the serving. Let's hope nothing unusual happens." They laughed together. Adam looked as though he wanted to kiss her, and strangely enough, she wanted the same.

She had to get off her feet, if only ten minutes. Florence removed her shoes and fell into the one comfortable chair, by the window. Peering out, she saw Ray removing something from the back of the Land Rover. It appeared to be a gasoline can, the kind her ex-husband used in the early days of their marriage to take to the station and fill with gas for the lawnmower. She shook her head in wonder; Ray was a strange man. Deidre' must have needed gasoline for something. She set the alarm on her phone, lest she doze off and miss the whole, shindig, as Ray called it. At five o'clock the alarm sound and she went into action.

At Safe Haven, T.J. and Elizabeth had gone into family conference. "He will. No, he won't." Jonathan and Nancy Ann heard raised voices, now and then, and shook their heads at sibling rivalry, wondering what the argument was this time. Nancy Ann gave Jonathan the once over and said, "I think I'll keep you." Jonathan smiled, as she stood before the mirror, applying make-up, with the towel wrapped around her body. "Yeah," he said, pulling her into his arms, "Then, that makes me think I will keep you." With one hand he was holding her close while the other unfolded the wrapped end of the towel. He was laughing as the towel fell to the floor. "You are such fun. If I hadn't found you, I'd be sitting in the sun in Florida pondering my demise."

Bobby was already herding his members into the church van. "Dear," his wife complained, "We are going to be the first one to arrive. That's not good. Let someone else win the prize." Bobby gave her a hostile look. "How did you know there's a prize?" To which she replied, "I always know, for you to get the whole group in the van without losing it, there's a prize." He looked a bit chagrined. "They couldn't figure out what to do with those little dolls Amy Moon makes, and I heard our ladies talking about Amy's expertise and how they wished they had one just to make a pattern off, you know, to make similar for their grandkids for Christmas?"

At the club, Joe glanced around, the setting was perfect. The Ensemble would sit to one side, the tables for those who wanted to visit were freshly adorned with white cloths and the new chandeliers lent the elegance he had always wanted. If people were dining out, give them a pleasant experience so they would come back. The only thing would have made it better was if Catrin was here. It was his solemn belief if he showered her with attention she would never stray. That led him to think of Elizabeth. Her Derek was to arrive home in time to attend the Event. Maybe it was just as well Catrin was in New York. They didn't need fireworks. He wondered how the horse and buggy deliverance from one facility to the next would go. Jud Arlin was ecstatic to showcase his prize beasts. Joe knew Jud practically kissed those animals' good night. They received better care than most husbands, certainly himself.

Back at the Inn, Terence lay on the bed. He couldn't get it out of his head that his dad was up to something. It worried him. He liked Miss Florence and Mr. Adam and Deidre' was his favorite. He'd read the text on his dad's phone. What could it mean? He tried to reform the words to memory. Ray, we put great trust in you that you won't let the sell throw you off the main purpose for visiting that area. It was with great conviction in your ability you were chosen to such an important undertaking; mainly to see that no one goes against what we are planning with the end result one we can live with for years to come. Terence tried to think, what were they talking about?

Like now, where was his dad? He'd left going to the next town, he said. For what? Why? Terence heaved a sigh. Deidre' offered he was to sit at head table with her, but he begged off, "let me wear a waiter's uniform and I'll be happy serving with the girls," he pleaded and won. At five forty five he would change into the black servers uniform and go down to help Deidre'.

Unknown to the group trying to save Deidre' and the Inn, two main players were on the way. One anticipated seeing his loved one. It seemed an eternity, but come December, they would be married and together forever. Finally. Derek smiled, moving his business from

California to Mosby, people would travel to discuss their need and Mosby Inn would have overnight guests. The other, smiled, to think Florence, was entering a new phase of life, one he hoped brought peace and happiness in her new surroundings, because she had always longed to return to the land of her youth. Life wasn't always hard work and struggle, he thought; there should be some fun along the way. The good Lord knew, in spite of troubled times, God had helped him see laughter was needed in a troubled world, lest one never see the sunrise or tell a loved one goodnight. She taught him that. Matthew smiled. His mother would be surprised to see him.

"What a task, Deidre'." Florence took in the table's gleaming silverware, the stemware, the china plates. "You have outdone yourself. It is beautiful and you are beautiful." She kissed the girl's cheek. "If I had a daughter, I would wish she were like you." Deidre' blushed and laughed.

Adam appeared. "Everyone's in their designated place and Houston, we are on go."

"You look dashing, Mr. Adam." Adam smiled and replied. "I wish our lady, agreed."

"I want to see the two of you dance. Terence told me the Club looks like a picture out of a magazine. I've not seen it since Joe put in the crystal chandeliers. It will be beautiful."

Putting his arm just so, Adam said to Florence, "Lay your hand there, my darling. It seems not our chariot awaits, but the tasks lie before us we agreed to. See, yonder the people are arriving." With that, he winked at Deidre' and led Florence to the foyer where they were to greet and chat with the guests. "Don't break a leg," he whispered in her ear, "and do save all the dances for me when we go to the club. Remember, you and I must ride in the same chariot."

She laughed. "I know you made that up."

"Did I tell you; you look ravishing? Did you notice my tie matches the color of your gown."

"You really are full of it, tonight."

"Only for you, my darling. Only for you."

Nancy Ann and Jonathan joined them in the receiving line. "I must say, you look great, Fleur." "The dress looks much better without the leggings." The two giggled and the men raised eyebrows. "You don't look so bad, yourself," Fleur replied. "I wondered what you had hidden in that closet." She hugged Nan. "I love you and I love how you look, all bridish." Nan blushed and Jonathan laughed. "Our men look rather fetching, too," Nan said, to cover her embarrassment. Fleur nodded, "Adam mentioned his tie matches my, or," she whispered, "your dress. What do you think?" Jonathan interrupted. "Girls, you are going to have to straighten up, we have to meet and greet these people and they are lined up to the number of one hundred sixty, outside that door, so pull it together." He and Adam shook hands in agreement.

"I'm nervous," Fleur admitted. "And I forgot to tell you, Marge won't be here."

"Oh? She did say she thought she was getting a cold, and why are you nervous?"

"I will tell you later. The reason may shock you." Nan gave her an incredulous look. "Yeah."

Nancy Ann just blinked. "I thought you and I were beyond being shocked. We aren't?"

The people kept coming, filling the tables after a stop at the door to view the list and find their name tag and table number. "Thank goodness you knew to add the table number to their name tags or we'd be here tomorrow," Fleur whispered. "I think there's more than a hundred sixty people." Nan asked, "What's the capacity?" Fleur whispered back, "two hundred and fifty." Nan blinked. "We could never have emptied tables quickly enough for the second half of the event." Fleur nodded, "Thank goodness for Elizabeth being aware we did have a pending problem."

It was at that moment, Elizabeth walked in with her Derek and Florence almost melt down when she saw who was following them. The young man saw her and came straight to her. "Mother?" He put a kiss on her cheek and hugged her.

"Matthew?" Florence didn't know if she was happy or in a complete state of shock. "Darling, what are you doing here?"

He grinned foolishly. "You sounded so bereft on the phone the day you left a message, I had to drop everything and come see about you and here you stand looking like a million."

Elizabeth was beaming at Nancy Ann. "Hey, Ma, he made it." Derek leaned across to kiss a smiling Nancy Ann on the cheek. "I guess we will l have wedding bells soon, after all."

"I'm bewildered," Florence was saying. "Nan, Elizabeth, this is my son, Matthew."

"We met outside," Elizabeth replied. "I know his name but we had not reached the part of who he belonged to." She extended a hand, "Glad to meet you. This is my fiancée, Derek."

"What a home coming," Nancy Ann whispered. "Fleur, are you going to introduce your son to Adam?" The two friends of a lifetime, shrugged away anyone or anything around them and stared at each other, what seemed like an eternity. "I guess I will," Fleur said, as dumbstruck as she had been in a very long time. "Just don't have them stand side by side," Nancy Ann said.

"How do I manage that?" Florence, asked, staring up to heaven. "Thank God, Adam and Jonathan walked away before this catastrophe." Elizabeth turned back, "I'm sorry, I didn't get that."

Nancy Ann pat her daughter's shoulder. "Take Matthew with you, will you? My number is by yours and Derek's, please remove my name and add Matthew's and do get acquainted. Okay?"

Florence was involved with more guests and as Nancy Ann digest the situation, she thought her friend was doing remarkably well. Until she heard her say. "Yes, we are so glad you could attend. Thank you, now do drive careful going home." It wasn't time to go home.

"It's a joke," Nancy Ann explained to the confused couple, "she means enjoy the night and do stay around for the horse and buggy ride up the hill after dinner, where there will be music and dancing, and then be careful on the way home." The couple laughed, and said, "we get it."

Somehow, Florence was able to avoid introducing Matthew to Adam while people streamed through the doors. The men had taken the position to make everyone who attend, feel appreciated. Bobby was for the most part tied up with his church group. "To each his own," Nancy Ann quipped, taking a glass of bubbly sprite from a huge tray. "If this were whiskey, I'd feel more equipped to talk to the men, but then, I'm jumping ahead, that's your worry." Fleur, gave her a pleading look and headed for the bathroom.

"This place is jivin." Adam came to stand by Florence. "Are you ready for the ride up the hill?" Florence had watched to see if Elizabeth and Derek included Matthew in their group and breathed a sigh of relief when the three turned to wave, before putting on their coats and going through the double doors to Jud Arlin's new enterprise. Adam and Jonathan were discussing how many people were left and decided it would be the logical thing if they, as hostess, went ahead. "How many people thought to bring a blanket?" Nancy Ann asked, "For the horse and buggy ride?" The men laughed. "More than you would have thought, thanks to the weather."

"But," Adam corrected, "Jud did say, he washed up all those he keeps in the buggy and you have to agree, the people came dressed for a party, which proves Mosby doesn't have many extravaganza's and they wanted an impressionable evening out."

"Deidre's dinner was marvelous. She and her cook did an amazing job. Now, to see how Elizabeth's boss comes across on his end of the deal," Nancy Ann commented. "It seems we made a wise decision letting the Ensemble set up one time, at Joe's. If the people missed live entertainment throughout the dinner, I didn't hear any remarks."

"I believe people are ready to leave the snow behind. You know, it's been dangerous to drive. But," Jonathan laughed, "there's just so many days active people can take being inside."

Arriving up the hill, beautiful music was pouring out the open doors as people entered Joe's club. "Wow." Florence was first to embark, holding on to Adam's arm, so she wouldn't miss a step on the ice. "It is beautiful, I don't think I even noticed the night I came up for the Inn, to bring back bottles of water. That seems a year past, and it was only the last snow storm."

"What in the world made you do that when there must have been capable men?" Nan asked.

"One man, as I recall," Florence replied. "Ray. And, on that night he was Mr. Grumpy."

Once inside, the men took the women's coats. The music was drawing people onto the floor and Matthew came for his mother. "Let's show 'em what its about," he said, grinning. "They have no idea what a young chick like you can do." Looking somewhat like a deer, captured in bright headlights, Florence let her son lead on to the floor.

They started out slow, Matthew's arm around her shoulder, side by side and then they went in to the usual foot action, as expert together as if soaring across ice and then, the song graduated to

Uptown Funk. It was easy to see Florence had taught Matthew from an early age, they were practically gliding across the floor. Adam was watching as he stood beside Deidre. She had quickly changed into a fitted bodice dress that was lilac in color and swirled to a full skirt just above her knees. "Let's do it," Adam said, "and after a round, we swap off? I'll take Florence and you take the guy that's dancing with her now."

"Oh, Mr. Adam, I'm not that good." But he was smiling and she would do anything for him.

"Sure, you are," he replied, "You just haven't found the rhythm, yet. Here we go." It was a few minutes later, as he said, they tapped the two on the shoulder and changed partners.

"Hi, I'm Deidre. Who are you? Matthew? Oh, okay, hope you don't mind the switch of partners. Not at all? Great." Deidre believed she had found her rhythm.

"Hello, Beautiful," Adam found Fleur light as a feather in his arms. "You haven't changed."

"I haven't?" She grinned. "Then why am I finding silver threads in my hair, now days?"

He laughed. "I hadn't noticed. I did notice you and the young man danced as though you have been doing it all your life. That tells me you have kept dancing through the years. Remember, we danced in the apple orchard and you said you hoped to dance forever."

"That was a long time ago," she said, a lump catching in her throat. She remembered. Oh, how she remembered, he had said, "on our fiftieth wedding anniversary we will come out and dance in the apple orchard." For a moment, she wished she could lay her head on his shoulder.

For a minister, Jonathan was a smooth dancer. "I wasn't always a good boy," Jonathan explained. "Before my calling, I loved the concerts and the dance off's." He smiled. "If you think dancing will send us to hell, we should stop, but I think if its done in the right place, with a partner God approves of, its little more than good exercise." His wife was nodding agreement.

"The only thing," Nancy Ann replied, "I'm going to be so sleepy, after all this."

"What's new about that?" He drew her closer to his body. "Have I told you today, I love you?"

When the huge grandfather clock that was Joe's parents, counted off eleven bass notes that probably could have been heard at the Inn, Joe ask several to come to the center of the room. "Deidre. Florence. Nancy Ann. Bobby. Adam. Jonathan. Terence." He searched the room for Terence but the young man did not come forward. "As you know, tonight's Event was planned to bring awareness to our community that there are times we need to stand together, in order to get our message out to the world, we are here. We have talented people with skilled crafts. We want to be recognized in our community and along the Interstate. The Inn, needs to grow and stay in Mosby, not move away and our people that would frequent our shops and village has a place to spend the night. Deidre,' you did a beautiful job with tonight's dinner."

The applause was deafening. "This is the group that organized the whole thing. I am standing behind those who worked so hard. Let's give them a hand. And last but not least, put your hand beneath the table and there should be a number you can match with a row of free gifts in the room next to the foyer, as you leave tonight, our way of saying thank you for supporting your community, your shops and each other. God bless you. There's one last song before you step out into the cold where the carriages are waiting. The horses are tired, but they will deliver you back to your vehicles. Thank you for coming to Deidre's Event."

The ensemble swung into Should Auld Acquaintance Be Forgotten and Joe was singing at the top of his voice. One old time resident passed by Adam and stopped to say, "You know, Adam, sometimes the apple doesn't fall far from the tree." A puzzled Adam, nodded and said, "yes."

"One last dance," was heard, as couples stepped out onto the floor. Adam reached for Florence hand. Those dancing seemed serene and lost in the moment of a good night together.

"Fleur," Adam's eyes held with Florence. "Please, Fleur, reconsider. There's nothing I want more, than to build a life with you. You know you belong here in my arms. Please, Fleur." The song ended and there was a jostle of going home. Florence didn't say a word. She merely pat Adam's arm, and said, "not now, please." Adam had no idea why she would say, not now.

A number of people chose to walk back to the Inn and their cars, those in appropriate dress, but Florence ankle length dress and matching shoes were not the given choice for walking. She and Adam climbed into the last buggy. "I have no idea where our Nancy Ann and Jonathan are," Adam said, arranging the blanket over Fleur. They had crossed the Club lot and headed a straight shot on the path to the Inn, when Adam asked, "Is that fog? It seems dense." And then, he sniffed the air and said in alarm, "Oh, no, it's smoke, and only the Inn lies ahead."

Florence felt something lurking in the back of her mind, but she could not pull it up.

Chapter 14

Nearing the clearing of the Inn's Parking Lot, people were scrambling to get in the cars. Those staying at the Inn, were frantic to reach their room, hoping the smoke had not overcome and flames that were leaping at the sides of the building on the outside were not also inside.

Deidre' had arrived in the first group, hoping all had gone well with the newly hired girl behind the desk to take new arrivals and deal with any of the guest deciding to leave due to weather coming in again, over the mountain. Seeing Adam and Florence, Deidre' cried out, "Mr. Adam, Miss Florence, what should I do?" She ran toward them, flinging herself into Adam's arms.

"Are there active flames, Deidre'?" Adam had his hands at her elbows, forcing her to face him. "Think, dear. What did you see and is there chance of a fire truck coming this far?" She was shaking her head, adamantly. Adam looked to Florence, for a measure of confidence. She was leafing through a small notebook, for information, he hoped. "No likelihood of help this far out, but around back there's a sustainable water resource and a huge water hose with a promised ability to reach one hundred feet in length. "let's check it out," Florence said and turned toward the back of the building. "But your shoes, your dress," Deidre was saying. "Your nice dress pants, Mr. Adam." Deidre' was like an old victrola, her voice was winding down.

"Where's the young man that was by your side as you were leaving?"

Deidre' gaped at Adam as though he had two heads. "I don't know, just like Miss Florence, when he saw the smoke, he took off running toward the back…just like she did, as though they know where the big water resource is, where we catch the rain and the run off from laundry and such, in case we ever need it…" She slumped against a small tree… "like we do right now, I guess." She needed to go into the Inn and help the people, strangely she could not move. She had been up since four that morning, the stress of cooking enough food to feed so many was heavy on her mind, and then she had to plan how to change clothes to go to Joe's club and foolishly, she had danced too many dances with a complete stranger. She was burnt out.

"Deidre'." Someone was calling her name. The new guy that danced with her as often as he could. Matthew. Matthew. "Deidre'," his voice demand she pay attention. "Tell those people to move the cars parked on this side of the building, or we are going to hose them down, so they don't go into flames, too." Deidre' stood gaping at Matthew. That's when he came close and grabbed her. His arms around her body, he began to shake her. "Come on, Dee, you are stronger than this. Forget it's a fire; think of it as a normal day. Come on, come out of it."

She began to cry. Total exhaustion mixed with shock was folding her body. The next thing Matthew knew, the new girl in his life was hanging from his arms lifeless. An elderly man and woman were coming toward him. "What's wrong with Deidre'?" They held his attention, with accusing eyes. "Son," the man asked, "did you do anything to her? That's one of the hardest working young women we will ever meet. So, what did you do."

Matthew was finding it hard to use his own hands to try to get Deidre' to stand, at least do something on her own. She wasn't heavy, but she wasn't helping him keep his balance, she was out of it. "Sir, if you would just help me, take her somewhere," he gasped. "She's exhausted."

"Bring her over here. We have one horse and buggy left for me and the Missus to ride home. My employees took the others in to put away for the night." He started walking toward the edge of the lot. Once arrived at the buggy, he opened the back gate and motioned to the floor. "Just lay her there and we'll cover her with the blanket. She'll be all right and if she doesn't wake up, we'll take her home with us."

Matthew ran back to where the big hose lay to find the man that danced with his mother, stretching it out, from where it had hardened in rounds. "I'll pull it forward, if you can turn on the water when I get it farther." Matthew nodded, "Just holler when you're ready." In a few minutes, Adam hollered, his arm up waving to Matthew. "Turn it on." Matthew returned to his side. "Should I go inside in case there are people asleep that didn't attend the Event?" Adam was busy with the hose. "What do you think caused this? I didn't see any equipment, that could have been faulty, actually there's no equipment on this side at all."

"I don't know, things happen." He tried to gauge the age of the young man. "You have a handkerchief, or something you can put over your face, going in, in case there's fire inside?" Matthew shook his head. Adam glanced down at himself, "I don't have any-thing, either, Just be careful. Smoke in the lungs is a bad one, too." Thinking what to do, he peeled off his jacket. "Here, put this on and when you enter, pull the front up over your face, maybe it will help."

Matthew did as was said but came running back almost imme-diately. "I see what happened, but it wasn't equipment. I think some-one set a fire there and it got to close to the building. I'm surprised they could even start a fire in this weather. As far as anyone inside, there's a door locked and no one answered. If there's a problem, it would be smoke inhalation."

"You take care of the water hose; I'll go see if I can open the door." Once more the water hose was transferred. Adam started back to the Inn, making note at any minute the electricity could shut down. He found the locked door and kicked with his foot; the lock held. Using his body, he rammed the door and heard a splintering sound. He pushed the door, allowing the broken lock to fall to the floor. There were two beds. The first was covered in bed spread, but the second had rumpled covers and in the bed was a girl, he guessed her age fourteen to fifteen with two little ones wrapped in each other's arms he guessed to be three or four years old. He couldn't imagine the parents leaving them, unless they were in off the Interstate and the parents left for supplies thinking the older girl completely responsible to be with the young ones. It was possible, sometimes parents did strange things.

Going to the back entrance he cupped his mouth and called out to Matthew. "Come help me." The young man laid the hose down and hurried to where Adam was planning to pick up the teenage girl. "There're two little ones in the next bed, see if you can manage them. Okay?" Matthew nodded and studied the two. If they would stay wrapped, he would be okay, but if they started squirming, he might not be able to hold on to them. There was something, the color green laying on the bed rail. He wrapped the piece of green around the little one's body and picked them up, one on each shoulder. "Good luck", the man said. Matthew smiled. He wasn't about to let those little fellows die in a fire. He and the man were of one mind.

Jud Arlin met Adam carrying the young girl. "Stand her on her feet," he told Adam. "I can't carry her but I can walk her to the buggy."

"There will be two little ones," Adam replied. "Make room for them." Matthew came toward them. His arms were full and amazingly the little ones were still asleep. Adam pointed to Mr. Arlin's buggy, and watched as the young man unloaded the two and returned to him.

"Do you think we need to walk through the hall and tap doors to be sure the rest are well?"

"Are you telling me, there's no smoke damage leaked into the second hall?"

"Not yet," the young man replied. He removed the jacket and handed over to Adam. "You may need this. Thanks."

Adam slipped the jacket on and started toward the back entrance again. "I believe you are right. We should check the rooms. I'll take the left hall North, you take the right. Agreed?"

An hour passed, the two speaking with the residents, explaining yes there was damage at the back entrance and smoke damage to the hall way but rooms closed off seemed to fare pretty well. Out on the lot, the cars had thinned out, the visiting Ensemble decided to go to their homes but the people who came over the mountain pass opted to stay if the smoke damage was not too intense in their room, and upon investigating, it wasn't and they stayed.

"I can't find Terence or his father," Deidre' informed them. "This is so unlike Terence."

"What about the Fire Marshall?" Adam was troubled no one had come to see what was needed for the people; clothes, food or anything of that nature.

Mr. Arlin asked about the girl's parents and her being guardian of the two small children. "We will take them home with us and take good care of them, if you want us to."

"How could a fourteen-year-old have guardianship?" A young man was asking. "Shh, his mother cautioned. "You just got here. These people were born here and you don't want to rile them.

"Actually" Adam replied, "the girl is eighteen and the little ones are three-year-old twins."

The boy seemed unable to drop the inquisition. "What are they doing out here?"

"Naturally, they were fine to stopping off at Mosby shops as one of the high lights when they took a round trip on the train," Adam explained. "Everyone loves train rides and crafts."

"We never dreamed of the excitement," the guardian remarked. "But we weren't hurt at all and we were never in the Inn." She smiled. "Now I find out if the little girls like me or not."

"But you have missed your train taking you back to wherever…" The boy was visibly perturbed.

"Thank you for caring," the girl said, softly. "We have to fend for ourselves all the time."

"My goodness," Nancy Ann whispered to Jonathan, "I hope everyone's as understanding."

"I understood there was to be a discussion concerning the Inn." Jonathan offered.

Nancy Ann looked lovingly at her husband. 'You care about everyone, too, don't you?"

"I do, but I don't want to hang around to hear every single person's complaint. It comes down to this, only the people connected to the Inn, have a voice. The rest made a choice."

Adam came toward them. "I heard you and I agree."

"Where's Fleur?" Now, Nancy Ann was worried. "She's likely to try to do something drastic, all by herself."

"Last I saw her, she was preparing to go to the other side of the Inn, check on the gathering room and try to cover every person that had reservation to stay over with a room. It seems only the back area was hit, smoke damage the most likely problem, in three or four rooms."

Jonathan gave Adam a curious glance. "That's not as bad as I thought. How do you think this started?" The question seemed to bring Adam to contemplate a thought back of his mind.

"I've not the foggiest." But there was something in the way the two stared at each other.

"Well, we are heading home. It was an interesting night. You might say something like this explains the old saying of strange bed fellows. I saw people dancing together, having fun, different ages and probably styles of life and I liked it." Yawning, he took Nancy Ann's hand and said, "Let's find our vehicle." He saw her reluctance. "I'm sure Adam will find Florence. Right?"

While they talked, the young man had rolled up the hose and placed just outside the storage room. It seemed he wanted to be certain, too, there were no loose embers. Glancing down, Adam saw not only the condition of the very ground where they had all walked and wondered how to help was a mix of crushed snow and ice mixed with mud, and ruefully he acknowledged so were his clothes. He should find Florence to tell her goodnight and go home.

* * * * *

Florence found an unsettled Deidre' and stayed with her until all rooms were secured and had been sprayed with some miracle name that said the product lived up to its words, that odor of any nature would be erased once the product was used, and they both prayed the words were true. Now, a very tired Deidre' came to plop down into the chair opposite Florence.

"Thank goodness, everyone had such a good fun time at the Event, they seem not to mind about their rooms. As long as their belongings were intact, they were fine." Suddenly she was astonished to see the grime settled into the lines and pores of her hands. "Oh, my poor hands."

Unknown to Deidre' the stranger in town had walked up behind her and when she put her arms up in the air, he captured them. "What's wrong with your hands?" Matthew laughed, "I was just thinking how you guided me through the dance, very well."

"Matthew, do you know this lady?" Deidre' rose to stand beside him. "She…"

"Of course, I do. I call her mom," he grinned, "or if I'm making a point and want her to listen, then I call her Mother. If you have forgotten, she and I were the first on dance floor."

Deidre' appeared shocked. "I didn't forget but I didn't know Miss Florence is your mother."

"You didn't." Both, Florence and Matthew were laughing. "I came unexpected. Sit, please and I'll join you for a minute and then we need to see if there's a room available." He smiled comfortably with the two. "I must say, you did have an exciting night. Does this mean everything is in good shape now, you can go forward. What do you think, Deidre'?"

"I'm worried, not just about tonight, but Ray said it is rumored there are new owners." She was tired and near crying. Florence and Matthew glanced at each other at mention of Ray.

Matthew saw sadness cross Deidre's face. "But why are you concerned? If you did this great job with the Event, you will do the unbelievable right here at Mosby Inn and with the new exercise equipment coming, many involved in a program will know you have the machines to continue and keep going." His gaze held hers. "Your color has come back. You were seriously pale and it was scary, but that older fellow with the horse and buggy seemed to know you so, I let him tell me what to do. Were you out long?"

"Was I out?" She seemed puzzled. "It was strange, waking up with two little people climbing over my body. I don't know if they are little boys or girls and their momma slept through it all."

"Where was this?" Florence was as confused as anyone. "This has been the most difficult day to understand. I won't even list the wrongs I know about. There might be new ones."

"Then, too, if there are new owners, will they like and accept me to stay on," Deidre' rambled.

Matthew gave his mother a searching look. "Haven't you told her?"

"Told her what, dear?" Then, she got his meaning. "I've not heard myself."

"I was told there was a gentleman supposedly headed this way to check out Mosby Inn. A company that owns several chains of motels throughout the country studied the Inn's location and with people expanding into obscure places, they felt it would be logical to check it out and have it ready for purchase." Deidre' listened her face seeming to change with each exchange of words, and then it was time, she knew she had to understand.

"Why am I getting the feeling the two of you know more about Mosby Inn, than me? It is as if you have some inner knowledge of it's future?" Her voice dropped off, the moment of bravery gone and what was following was a profound reasoning that she no longer had a job at Mosby Inn. "Miss Florence, did you come to Mosby Inn to investigate and see if it was worth keeping? Helping me under false pretense? All the while I thought you a good woman who saw my need for help because my serving girls couldn't make it in over bad winter roads?"

Florence gave a low groan. "Matthew, see what you've done?" She reached for Deidre's hand. "My dear, I helped you because you were worn out trying to do it all by yourself. Who did or did not own Mosby Inn had nothing to do with my joining you. You are a hard-working woman and I appreciate how dedicated you are to your job."

"But," Deidre' was insistent now. "I must know, do you know the new owners? Must I start looking for a new job?" She cast a miserable glance first to Matthew and then her eyes stayed on Florence. "It's winter, and I will have a hard time navigating these roads beyond Mosby." A new thought entered her mind. "But, now, with damage to the Inn, will your people even consider purchasing the Inn?" With fresh energy Deidre' rose up out of the chair.

Florence heaved a deep sigh. Suddenly, the whole thing seemed too much. "Why don't you tell us both, what you know, Mathew?"

"I'm puzzled, the two of you make my news appear as a problem." He turned to Deidre.' "My mother used to spend summer vacation here, in Mosby. Evidently, she never forgot it and when she heard the Inn was up for sale, she asked me to look into it. What I found, was, a large hotel chain was considering tearing down the Inn and building one of their own here." Deidre' appeared disheartened and sit down to let it all sink in.

"However, the man dealing with your boss, Galant, came across condescending and abrasive and Mr. Galant was non too pleased with his attitude, and it seems he doesn't have to rely on abrasive people and he turned down the rascal and sold the Inn to none other than your kitchen helper, my mother."

Tears formed to drip down Deidre's cheeks. She scrubbed at them, the film of black soot making obvious runs in the tears. "I apologize if I said anything rude. I'm so tired, I may have." Her voice was more of a whisper and Florence reached out to comfort her.

"Diedre', please, put your mind at ease. Tomorrow, we will look into the damage in daylight and you can rest assured, you are and will be the manager of Mosby Inn and I'm sorry we are hearing the news at such an inopportune time, but life is like that, so let's accept it as good news and tomorrow we will carry on." Florence hugged Deidre'. "I'm sorry for the anxiety this has caused you."

"Please don't be nice to me, I might cry."

Matthew aimed his phone, "Is this a good time to snap a photo of the new owner and manager of Mosby Inn?"

"Oh, no. No picture." Florence and Deidre' covered their face, as the door opened.

Adam arrived. "Thank God," he said. "I've spent the last hour looking for Deidre'. Mr. Jud said she disappeared and he, "couldn't go looking for her when he had to watch them little three-year-old twins." Adam laughed. "His words, his grammar. He takes his task to heart."

Matthew joined his laughter. "Our ladies here, have faced a startling bit of news for the night, beside the unexpected fire that ruined all of our fine evening wear, but I believe that's resolved. Now, ladies, do you have an extra room for a poor stranded city boy, like me?"

For a minute the two looked stricken as Florence looked to Deidre' for the answer.

"No, but I can clean my room for you," Deidre' stuttered. In a moment of bewilderment of another problem presenting its self, Florence thought to take advantage of the atmosphere, when she said, "Adam, I understand you and Matthew worked together putting the fire out and checked to see if it had spread to the rooms, but have the two of you officially met?"

"No, we haven't and I want to help out with the Inn having run out of rooms for this young man."

"Adam," Florence said, quietly. "I would like for you to meet my son. Matthew."

A smile made little crinkling's around Adam's eyes, as he offered his hand. "Just call me Adam. I have plenty of room at my house," he was saying. "No problem if you just come home with me." And Matthew shaking his hand, replied, "Matthew Bennett." If Adam made the connection to Matthew's last name being the same as his middle name, he didn't show it. "I don't know about you, but I'm ready to throw these clothes in the trash and have a clean shower. I'd say Deidre's event ended with a bang, and while it wasn't the right kind of bang to celebrate, I heard raving reviews of the evening being a success."

"Yes, it was a nice turn out." Matthew looked around, gearing up and ready to leave and was about to tell his mother good night, when he noticed Deidre' staring at him as he stood by Mr. Adam. "You all right, Dee?" She shook her head and turned toward the registration station. Her thoughts were so strong she was afraid her mouth might relay what she had seen and she could not help but wonder if Miss Florence saw it too? Mr. Adam and the young man she danced with, bore enough resemblance to be father and son. What a coincidence.

Adam kissed his mother on the cheek, but couldn't resist pulling her from where she sit on the edge of a table, to lock her in dance mode as he whirled her around the empty space, humming and singing, she'll be coming around the mountain, coming around the mountain, she'll be coming around the mountain at Mosby Inn."

"Oh, my, Son; I don't think I have enough energy left to dance at this time of night."

Adam was clapping. "I knew right off there had to be a connection between you two. You were that good together on the dance floor."

Releasing his mother, Matthew quipped, "You two weren't so bad, either. Any secrets you want to tell me?" His mother closed her eyes and Adam gave an embarrassed chuckle.

"Good night, Deidre', Florence," Adam was turning toward the door. "A great evening."

"I'll have to get my luggage from the vehicle." The women heard Matthew's words, followed by Adam's, "So you are the lucky guy driving that, huh?" Their laughter sounded in the night.

Florence watched as Deidre' opened the refrigerator and began counting how many dozen eggs she had for the morning breakfast and nodded satisfied there was enough bacon. Glancing at the wall clock behind the registration desk, Florence ask, "Shall we shower and get in clean clothes and start breakfast, or sleep a couple hours before we start?"

"Oh, Miss Florence, it doesn't make sense, if you are the new owner, you can't be helping me serve breakfast or clean the Inn."

Florence laughed. "Nothing's changed, Deidre', except more to do now that there was a fire."

Chapter 15

They arrived back to Chatham. Matthew was impressed, glancing around the landscape. "Hey, this is all right. A man could die here and think he was in heaven. Did you do this? The architecture?" Taking it all in, "Even an apple orchard. Now that's romantic. I suppose there's an old rock wall runs at the edge of it and somewhere in there will be a lover's bench, or is it a swing?"

"You got me," Adam admitted. "After the folks died, and I was at odds with life, I started changing things to the way I always saw them in my mind." He saw the question in the boy's mind. "Yeah, a failed marriage, you could say, loveless. She and I had no feelings for each other and she always loved another. I know. I know. Why? Right? I ask myself that a hundred times a year, but she did have a little girl that made life more bearable." He grinned. "You gotta watch out for those girls. No matter the age, they rope you in."

"I believe you. How about Dee? Does she have anyone?"

"Deidre'? No, not that I know of, maybe there was once, but I think he went Military."

"She seems nice and from what I saw tonight, a hard worker. I can't imagine getting up in the morning to make breakfast for how many was it, forty three people?"

"If you want, we will go down around eight and see what's going on."

"Good deal." Matthew followed Adam to the bedroom beyond the sitting room. "Nice," he said, as they walked though. Adam left him to discover what he needed by himself and finally as he sank on the pillow, he sniffed, thinking the pillow's fragrance remind him of his mother's perfume. Putting his hand under the pillow he touched a small object.

Adam was peeling the clothes from his body when he thought he heard a scratching sound on the ground balcony beyond his bedroom window. He listened, but decided it was a branch scrapeing the outer wall of the house and stepped into the shower, thankful for hot water. But later as he slipped into pajama bottoms, he heard movement outside the window, again. Pulling on a sweatshirt and finding his shoes, he went to the double doors, opened one and stepped out. Someone was laying beneath the silver tarps that covered the summer furniture.

Reaching inside the doors, he flipped the switch for the overhead light and pulled back the tarp.

"Terence?" The boy was scrunched up in a ball, and in spite of the cold, seemed to have been asleep. They were equally surprised to see each other. "Terence, what are you doing here?"

The boy pulled himself up and let his legs dangle off the chaise he lay on. "Mr. Adam?"

"Yeah, Terence, it's me. Did you know you were at my house sleeping on my furniture?"

For a minute Terence appeared ready to cry. "I didn't hurt anything. Honest. But I started walking away from the Inn and I ended up here. I guess I could have found my way back."

"I looked for you at the Event, but neither you or your dad was around. Everything okay?" He motioned for Terence to follow him inside. "Come on in. You could get a cold out there. Did you just decide to take a nap? For heavens' sakes, you know better than to do this in the winter." Terence was following him through the doors. "Have you had anything to eat or drink?"

Terence shook his head, "No, Sir. I just started walking when Dad left."

Adam gave Terence a strange look. "Well, I don't know where he was going but he hasn't returned, yet. I would have recognized his Land Rover on the lot."

"No, Sir, he won't be back."

Something in Terence voice made Adam stop, pulling bread and sandwich makings from the frig. "What do you mean he won't be back? He has to come back for you."

"No, Sir, I refused to go with him." A tear slid from Terence eye, rolling silent down his cheek. "I won't ride with him, when he's in one of those moods. We could get killed."

"Terence, your dad won't leave you." Trying to make sense of what the boy was saying, Adam shoved the food to the middle of the island in front of Terence, and began making a sandwich for him. "You like cheese?" Terence gave a nod. "Mayo?" Another nod.

"He may have to stay overnight on the other side of the pass, but he'll be back tomorrow."

"No, Sir, he won't. When he's upset about something, he takes his time."

"How much time?" Adam, squinch eyed, stared hard at Terence? "How much time is that?"

"Last time, he left me and Mom for three months. She had to get a job to make enough money to get us back home."

"Where was that, he left you?"

"We lived Oklahoma, then, but he left us in Indiana. We had no wheels. She had to work a month to make enough to make a down payment on an old clunker." A slight smile came into Terence eyes. "My Mom was as smart as she was pretty, and better than I'll ever be."

"I'm sorry you lost your Mom."

"Me, too. She kept us together, but Dad, he's foot loose and likes to do what he wants."

"So, has he left you often?" Thinking the boy probably wouldn't eat, Adam was surprised to see him wolfing down the sandwich. "You want me to fix you another sandwich?"

Terence nodded. "I hadn't eaten since early morning when me and Deidre' were cooking for the dinner and she wanted me to taste the beef special with some kind of brown gravy. It was good, too."

Silently, Adam thanked God for Deidre.' "Did she know you and your dad were having problems?"

"There was no way, she could have missed it. He got after her, about the Inn, said he'd been sent down here to see it was sold to the right people and he had a big bonus coming from the sale. It upset her and I told him the timing wasn't good with her trying to pull the event together." Terence, turned his head to look at Adam, and that was when Adam saw the right side of Terence face was bruised, that eye drooping a bit. "Dad didn't care what she had to do."

Thinking to give comfort, Adam said, "I wouldn't worry too much, he'll be back tomorrow."

"Don't count on it," Terence replied. "He's really upset with me. I told him I'm through with him." His eyes dropped to stare at his mirrored reflection in the black granite Island. "Mr. Adam, do you suppose I could stay with you, until I get enough money to make it on my own?"

"You realize your dad has a say in your whereabouts."

"You've not met a dad like mine. He takes care of himself and expects me to take care of me."

"I tell you what, there's a room upstairs. You take a look and see if you can handle it, and if you can, we will face your Dad when the time comes. Get some sleep and we'll talk tomorrow." Adam restored the food items and was going to his room when he asked, "Do you need anything? Clothes? Toothbrush, anything?"

"No, Sir, I have a hobo pack with me and the rest is in Deidre's laundry room at the Inn."

Adam tousled the boy's hair. "Everything will be all right, Terence. Some things just take time." He was almost to the door, when he said, "We'll go to the Inn, eight in the morning."

A bit weary, he climbed into bed, thinking, he had always wanted a son. Tonight he had two.

* * * * *

Terence was waiting by the truck when Adam came down the front steps, followed by a new guy. He was dressed country enough for Mosby, but there was something spoke city about him. Mr. Adam, said, "Good Morning, Terence. This is Miss Florence, son, Matthew." He looked back to see if Matthew was following. "This, fine fellow, Matthew is Deidre's best helper and we call him Terence." Adam chuckled as Terence mumbled "Hi," and Matthew, like a city slicker, said, "Good Morning." Terence climbed in the back seat and Matthew took the front.

"Well, Boys, no telling what we will find at the Inn this morning. If we need to pitch in and help, let's just do that. I may have made breakfast for ten or fifteen people in my life, but never forty-five or more." Adam glanced back to Terence, as he explained to Matthew, "If you need any help to know where something goes, Terence is your best go to."

"You must have an inside line, Adam." Matthew whistled. "I don't believe there were this many cars parked in the lot, last night. What's this about? When something happens, everyone comes to check it out?"

"Part of it, is Mosby could use a good restaurant but no one's been willing to invest. There's the Club on the Hill, but Joe is more into a nice dinner. Who knows, maybe we should think about that, build bigger and have a five-star restaurant attached to the Inn, that does breakfast and dinner." He could see Matthew's interest. "It has great potential, doesn't it?"

* * * * *

The gathering room was buzzing. Adam heard Terence say, "Come on, I'll show you what we do. Deidre's the best." He smiled to himself. He had already seen the two young people were drawn to each other. He found Fleur at the coffee station.

"Morning, darling Fleur." She gave him a squint-eyed look. "Need any help?"

"We're surviving. A group of ten are headed in. You can find a table for them, if you want." She noticed he was freshly groomed and the fragrance of his after shave smelled like a million. It gave her cold chills, it was the same as when he first started shaving. "You haven't changed after shave fragrance?"

"No," he smiled and winked, "I don't change, I stay with what I like best. Women in particular. Have you decided to marry me, yet?" She shook her head. "You will," he said. The group arrived and he seated them at the only window table left and was back with their order for coffee. "There's an older couple in the group celebrating fifty years. I don't think we can add fifty years, do you? But, let's see, we might make thirty. I'm ready. How about you?"

"You were such a quiet boy. What happened?" She poured coffee into each cup he presented. Their eyes met, and he was grinning like a foolish teen. "Stop oogling me, the people will notice." He winked and sighed. "How did you and my boy do together?"

"He is a nice young man. I enjoyed him in the short time we were together, but of course, Terence was with us this morning and we didn't talk much. You know Ray left him here?" She seemed stunned. "Yeah, he said his Dad is known for leaving him and his mother, but this time he told Terence he wasn't coming back. Terence is with me."

Florence laid a hand on Adam's arm. "Thank you. Terence is a really good kid. I've known from the beginning something was wrong, but I never figured it out." She gave a deep sigh, "It breaks my heart, a parent would abandon their child."

"I never had one." Adam seemed to think back. "Funny, as I lay down last night, after feeding Terence, I thought, I always wanted a son. Tonight, I have two." He laughed self-consciously. "Old men can dream dreams, can't they?" He moved on with the tray of coffee.

By mid-morning, the guests were clearing the gathering room and Adam, Matthew and Terence began the mop down, chairs on tabletops, sweep, mop, put back chairs, clean table with disinfectant. "Nice, job, Bro." Terence had warmed to Matthew "Now, I should retire, since I taught both of you the ropes to cleaning Deidre's kitchen. However," he eyed them both, quite serious as he walked around them, his hand to his chin, studying both. "I did notice, neither of you could keep your eyes off certain girls." Turning to Adam, he said, "Specifically, you talked a lot to Miss Florence. If you are thinking of asking her out on a date, now's the time, I can tell she is interested. Of course, I did hear her tell you to straighten up and I hope you did nothing outwardly, you get my meaning?"

Matthew bent over, laughing, but Terence turned his attention on the new-comer. "You, Sir, seem smitten with the beautiful hard-working Deidre.' I can tell you only one thing. She rests for an hour before starting preparation for the evening meal. During that hour, if permissible, she loves to take a walk. You might pay close attention to the little details." With that, Terence hand the broom over to Matthew and said, "I believe we are finished. Time to put away tools."

* * * * *

At loose ends, Adam found Fleur. "I was wondering if you would like to take a ride?"

"Would I be asking to much of you, to stay an hour or so, as the insurance person is on the way to discuss and view the damage to the rooms and to try to find the reason for the fire."

"No, I'd be glad to stay. Why don't we go out and give it a look, before the person arrives?" He heard Terence in the background asking Deidre if she had seen his bundle of clothing, as he followed Fleur out the back entrance and around to the side of the building most damaged.

"It's just a mess," Fleur was saying, studying the wall charred down to the foundation. "There's no electrical box, only the usual thread of necessary wires and this lump of something, I guess it's insulation." She sighed. "I'm not good at this. What's your opinion?"

"Wait for the expert." One hand to an elbow, he guided her to a wooden bench that someone had raked the snow away and was decently dry. "Let's sit a minute."

At that moment, his cell rang. "Shall I leave?' Fleur whispered. "No," he motioned, "Stay."

"Dad? This is Amy." Adam's breath caught sharply. "Amy? Is something wrong?"

"No, Dad, I can't put up with Mother. I'm coming home." Amy laughed. "Don't be shocked Dad. I know you haven't heard from me, but I never forgot Poppa that read all the books to me."

"You didn't?' He felt like the air had stopped coming through his body. "When will you be here?"

"Tomorrow, Dad. Is my room still there?" She listened as he grunted, "See you tomorrow, Dad," and then the line went silent. Were those tears in his eyes? Who died?

"You look like you've seen a ghost." She lay a hand on his arm. "Are you all right?"

"That was Amy." He blinked, trying to clear his mind along with his eyes. "I didn't know I missed her so badly. Hearing her voice, I wanted to cry."

"I think you did. Adam, I didn't know you were this soft hearted."

"Except, for you. You knew, I was for you." She smiled. "Yeah, I knew you knew my feelings."

"What has happened?"

"She's coming home." He seemed in a stupor "I wanted to ask you again, will you marry me?" His eyes locked on her, as his hand came up to smooth a few loose strands of hair that had strayed outside the knitted cap she wore. "Suddenly, I have Terence and here comes Amy, and what woman wants a fully made family, not of her own doing." He laughed, embarrassed. "Why don't we just all move in together? Maybe Matthew would like to stay." He smiled. "I really like your son, Fleur, but if he is part of you, why wouldn't I?"

"You have a family and I have just learned I got the Inn, an Inn that suffered damage just as it comes into my hands. Would you want that on your plate along with your new family members?"

"If you are part of the deal, Fleur, I would consider it a great bargain." He slipped down on one knee, his eyes pleading. "Fleur, would you consider marrying me? I need a mother figure in my household, but most of all," he sighed. "I find I'm so weary of being alone, always my mind thinks of you." He started to rise. "Would you consider what I've said?"

"Yes." Fleur sat there, studying the face she'd dreamed of a million times. "Yes. I will."

"Yes, to which part?" He asked as he settled down beside her. "The part of being the mother figure, the part of me getting older, or being my wife?"

"Yes." Confused, he turned to study her expression. "Yes." A smile was brightening her face.

"You will consider?"

"I said, yes. Yes, I will marry you. You do need a mother figure if you're going to raise kids."

"And not one of them mine," he said sadly. "You know I always wanted us to have a child."

"We will." She laughed, suddenly years of being tied down, doing what she had to do not what she wanted to do, were too much, always conforming. "We will."

"Aren't we a little old for that?" He seemed bewildered. "You are going to marry me?" He grinned. "Well, good." He grabbed her and kissed her. "But we can't have a baby."

"We already do, but he's past twenty years old." The minute of time seemed an eternity.

It was like lightning in a dark sky when he realized what she meant. His eyes brightened. He pulled her up and they did a dance around the bench. "You mean?" He was laughing joyously. "Now, I get it. The night of the Event, so many people said, "Adam, the apple sure didn't fall far from the tree. When I said, what do you mean. They just laughed. They meant Matthew, didn't they? I dismissed it, but once when he was talking to Deidre' I remember comparing him to a photo my mother kept of me, when I was about that age."

"We may have to approach this cautiously."

"He doesn't know?" Fleur shook her head. "Will he be upset?"

"I don't know." She felt a smidgen of worry. "He thinks he never had a real daddy."

"The man you married, wasn't father material?" She shook her head.

"I thought he would be but I was wrong, and as a husband, he was a skirt-chaser."

"We've waited over twenty years, Fleur. I don't see a reason to wait any longer. Why don't we call Jonathan, tonight." There were tears in Fleur's eyes, "after we talk to Matthew. Okay?"

* * * * *

Terence gave a sharp whistle, gaining Matthew's attention as he was putting on warm clothing to go out into the cold. "Over here," Terence hissed. "You gotta see this. It's not the first time, I saw Mr. Adam go down on his knee in front of her another time. I ask him was he asking forgiveness or proposing and he ignored me. But get a load of this. Whatta you make of it?"

Matthew joined him at the window. What he saw was Mr. Adam rising to sit beside his mother on the bench. "They are old friends, you know." Terence gave him the look. "Yeah," Matthew agreed, "it looks like something important is going on." He turned hearing the back door open and close, "that's Deidre'. Right? I gotta go, if I'm going to join her for that walk."

"Aren't you interested in what's happening out there, with your mother?"

Terence heard the reply, "it's not as though Mr. Adam is a predator, friend." The door closed on Matthew's laughter and a second later he saw through the window, Matthew joining Deidre.

* * * * *

"You like Mr. Adam?" Deidre' gave him a strange look. "Oh, yes. I mean, good morning to you and how are you after all that busy breakfast hour. We didn't get a chance to talk.'

"Hi." She started down the path, past the parking lot and on to rows of hedge covered in ice and snow. Her boots made gushing sounds where there were holes that held water beneath the ice. Sliding once, he caught her hand to keep her upright. "Thanks."

"Why so quiet?" He held tight to the hand she was trying to remove. "I like you. I admire you. I think you're pretty." He laughed. "How's that for getting acquainted?"

"Why do you want to know if I like Mr. Adam?" She glanced his way and once more felt there was some connection between him and Adam Chantham. "He's a fine man, a gentleman and I respect him more than any other man I know."

"Has he earned that respect?"

"Yes." She began by telling him the times Adam had sensed her problems and without telling him what they were he had eased her pain and give her encouragement to keep going. "It has been difficult here at the Inn, but I love this place and I love my job. So, yes, it's good to have people like Mr. Adam in my life, when I have no one else."

Matthew stopped, not turning loose her hand. She was forced to face him, waiting for whatever was heavy on his mind. "I know we are strangers, but I do like you, Dee, and I have a crazy feeling we are going to get to know each other so well, that one day we will laugh about today. What do you see when you look at me and then you look at Adam?"

She was hesitant. He was waiting. "Dee, say it. What do you see. Tell me I'm not crazy."

* * * * *

The day passed without incident, other than Terence could not find his belongings left in the laundry room at Mosby Inn. He and Deidre' had searched diligently, to no avail. It was to her dismay she finally offered, "some of the guests must have taken them by mistake." Within the next hour as Florence met with the Insurance agent and he ask why there was a pile of clothing lying alongside the charred back wall of the motel, with the appearance someone had chosen to burn on the spot, they then decided Terence father had destroyed his son's personal items.

"What kind of father, does that?" Deidre' asked, sadness in her eyes. Privately, to Terence she said, "I'm very sorry, if I hurt your feelings. It just slipped out." Terece assured her it was the kind of thing his father would do. Thinking to lighten the moment, she asked, "Would you like to ride with me to Miss Nancy Ann's? Tomorrow night? She has sent an invitation for all of us to come for dinner. A chili or soup dinner, as I understand." She smiled and hugged him. "You can have a room here at the Inn, if you want, since the guests are leaving. Think about it."

* * * * *

Matthew studied the painting over the mantel. Adam watched the boy. His mind correcting, he had to think of him as a young man, a business man in his own rights. He had negotiated the purchase of Florence buying the Inn. His boy. Somehow the pride he felt in the young man was more than the worry the boy's mother was experiencing in finding a perfect time to tell the news to their son. Son. Somehow, he couldn't help but smile at the thought of calling Matthew, son.

"Am I right? The woman in that painting reminds me of photos I've seen of mother at that age. Was she even twenty at the time?" He glanced across at Adam, watching him.

"It is your mother. She sit for the artist. The painting set in Marge's store window, down at the shops, and I bought it to replace the most ridiculous painting ever that my mother's decorator had hung there. Do you like it?"

"I find it interesting." With that, Matthew rose up and paced the floor, finally to say what was on his mind. "My mother is now owner of the Inn. I believe she will be happy here as she has nothing or no one other than me to tie her to another place. I'm thinking of relocating, here." Now he turned to Adam's attentive expression as he listened. "What would you think of that? Does it make any sense, at this age, I'd like to be near my mother?"

Adam's pleasure was evident. "I think that would be wonderful." It was then, Adam's cell rang. "Excuse me, I'll need to get this." With discomfort he answered, "Charlotte?" He listened to her discourse and at the closing of their conversation, he said, "I take it, you have talked Amy out of coming to live here? Yes, I realize she is finishing college for a second degree. It's her choice, Charlotte. Yes. Yes. She can call me anytime. I'm glad the two of you are in agreement."

"That's life," he said. "Yesterday, my ex-wife's child called saying she was coming here to live. Today, her mother I've not spoken with in years, tells me otherwise. Life changes, one day at a time." His eyes held with Matthew's. "I pray, you do stay and we form a beautiful relationship."

The snow storm that came that day was unannounced by the weather man and seemed to hit hardest in the area between Stiger Mercy Mountain Pass and the Interstate Visitors station three miles East of the small tourist stop, Mosby. Stranded and unable to go beyond the area, guests piled in to Mosby Inn, unmindful of the renovation that had begun and was now halted. The lives of the community inhabitants changed that day. Strangers off the Interstate wandered the shops section, purchasing and making plans to have the purchase shipped to homes across the states and Mosby became a place on the map, listing quality items people would treasure.

Matthew was thrown into the company of his mother's friend's family. He was invited to be a best man at Elizabeth and Derek's wedding, standing with Deidre, making his mind speed ahead; their own romance would bloom and present in time, the same idea of being together. He was happier than he could remember, in years. Seeing his mother and Adam together, he wondered if they would ever get around to telling him the words he longed to hear.

It was a day when T.J. and Terence were working on the snowmobile, he and Adam managed in the four-wheel drive to pick up his mother from the Inn and make it down the lane to Nancy Ann and Jonathan's home. It was when the conversation lulled after a stomach filled chili dinner, perfect to fit the weather, and all were gathered, that Matthew thought he could stand it no longer. Just as he wanted to speak up, his mother motioned him near.

"Son," she said, "could you and Adam and I go in to the other room? We have something we need to discuss with you?" Matthew glanced to the sound of the front of the house, his heart leaping in relief that Deidre' had made it up the lane, no doubt in ruts as deep as a car's tires, but she was here and he had a feeling they were about to hear words to change his life forever. Neither Adam or Florence questioned Matthew claiming Deidre' and bringing her along.

They settled in Nancy Ann's small sitting room, waiting. Finally, Florence spoke, "Matthew, I find it difficult to tell you, what I must. After all the years, you wondered who your father was, and you wanted a father, but that part of our life was not to be, until now." At that, Florence began to weep. "I'm happy to tell you, but it's so hard for me. I don't know what you'll think."

He could stand it no longer. Going to his mother, he slid down in front of her. He was almost laughing as with one hand on her knee, he reached into his pocket and brought out a small brown bottle, she recognized immediately, but a puzzled frown came across her brow.

"Mother, this little pill bottle was never out of your possession. I bet you've searched for it a hundred times since you left it under the pillow at Adam's house. You slept in that bed, once, didn't you?" He grinned. "Does Adam even know? Because he never mentioned it." He was aware Adam rose to stand by the fireplace. Pain for Fleur was evident in his expression.

"No." She whispered, her head falling to her chest. "Yes, the night he carried me from the chasm, I had not taken my meds and they told me to stay there or go to hospital."

"Mother, what do you have to tell me? That I'm the spitten image of my father? That you want to marry him after all these years but you have this grown son, you don't know what to do about?" He put his arms around Florence. "Just say it, Mother. Who is my father?"

Adam's heart was bursting. He came to the two, settling down on the small sofa by Fleur. "I didn't know about you, Son. I'm glad I'm your father. I only learned of you when you arrived unexpected for Deidre's Event. Actually, it was the people's remarks about our looking like each other set off my curiosity as to what they meant, but I had already asked your mother to marry me."

"I can imagine. She said no, didn't she?" Matthew grinned. "Mother always has to have everything in place." He hugged Florence, again. "Mother, what do you want to say?"

"Adam is your father. We loved each other but fate got in the way. It was only before we parted, we spent the night together and he never knew I was pregnant with his child."

Matthew rose up. "Well, now he knows and I know and even Deidre' knows." He offered a hand to Adam, pulling him up. "Oh, no," he said, "not just a handshake. I've waited twenty three years for my father to hug me."

Adam put his arms around his son. "Dad," Matthew said. "This feels like home."

Adam was the one explained, to the group of friends. Within the hour, the snow laden day became a day of celebration. "We plan to marry as soon as the snow melts and we can get a license," Adam said, smiling and holding Florence hand. "Thank you all for your good wishes. It means a lot to us.

Nancy Ann beamed. She and Florence had come a long way, she with her son by another mother. She glanced to where T.J. was taking it all in. He winked at her. She noticed Elizabeth and Derek, holding hands as they sit in front of the fireplace. They were going to make the Valentine Day wedding after all. And Jonathan. How did God know she needed Jonathan?

Florence heart was happy to bursting. So, Matthew had found the little brown pill bottle and pieced it all together. He was a good son and his father a good man. She prayed they had years to build a firm foundation. She felt Adam's eyes rest upon her and looked up. I love you, he mouthed, silently and she smiled. This was what she had waited a life time for, Adam's love, his presence in her life. Thank you, Heavenly Father, she thought, silently as the peace that passes all understanding settled upon her.

Who would know? A heart waits, forever

And sometimes prayers are answered.

THE END

Books by Betty Lowrey

PROMISES

FORGIVEN

FORBIDDEN

FORSAKEN

FOREVER

FORGOTTEN

SECRETS

WHEN SOMEBODY LOVES YOU

FOR THE LOVE OF STORMY WEATHER

LOVING YOU ALWAYS

WHEN DREAMS COME TRUE

WHERE THERE'S LOVE

WHEN YOU CALL MY NAME

ENGRAVED ON MY HEART

WHEN MY HEART SINGS

A HEART TWICE BLESSED

FAITH IN SPITE OF THE STORM

BARKLEY

LILY

EMMA

AMANDA

OUR HEARTS COME HOME FOR CHRISTMAS

A HEART WAITS FOREVER (2024)

www.ingramcontent.com/pod-product-compliance
Lightning Source LLC
Chambersburg PA
CBHW051232130726
47988CB00001B/320